DESERT DOCTOR

MEDICINE
AND EVANGELISM
IN THE KALAHARI DESERT

DESERT
DOCTOR

ALFRED M.
MERRIWEATHER
C.B.E., M.D., F.R.C.P.(Ed.), D.T.M. & H.

LUTTERWORTH PRESS
GUILDFORD AND LONDON

First published 1969
This impression 1974

Lutterworth Press, Luke House,
Farnham Road, Guildford, Surrey

ISBN O 7188 1637 4

Printed in Great Britain by Fletcher & Son Ltd, Norwich

CONTENTS

FOREWORD

I am glad to be able to write this short Foreword to Dr. Alfred Merriweather's book about his medical and evangelistic work in my country, Botswana.

Dr. Merriweather's long service to Botswana is well known, and in his book he gathers together a splendid range of incidents, stories, and events which illustrate the wide range of his activities.

We in Botswana value him for what he has done and is doing for our people, and I hope his book will have the wide circulation it deserves.

STATE HOUSE,
GABERONES.

SERETSE KHAMA
President of Botswana

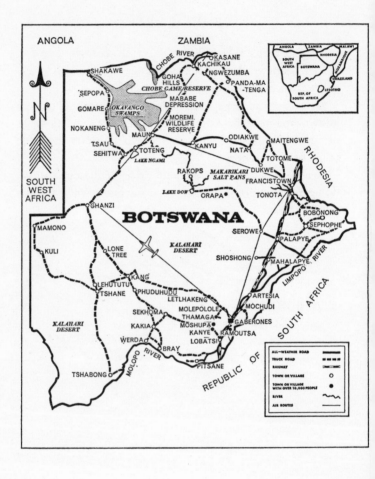

I

WHERE THE KALAHARI DUST BLOWS

I drove the Bedford truck out of the hospital grounds, down the rough, gravel road into the sprawling town of Molepolole. Morwakgosi had cycled up to the hospital and asked me to go to see his child, very ill, at Tshosa's place. He had thrown his bicycle on to the back of the truck, which served as an ambulance, and in order to guide me to the hut sat beside me in the cab of the truck. We chatted freely together, in Setswana, as black and white do in this multi-racial Republic of Botswana.

Morwakgosi was natural and polite without any sign of inferiority or racial prejudice. He called me 'Mokwena', 'one of his tribe', and I called him 'Rramaria', meaning 'father of Maria'. Maria was his first-born child and I called him, according to custom, after his first-born child.

It was an afternoon in early October, and in a week or two the rains would come, if God so willed and if the Bakwena did not make him angry. Now before the rains, the early summer heat was intense, and my shirt stuck to the cab seat with the perspiration which poured from me. On my exposed arms and legs the sweat evaporated immediately into the hot, dry air, leaving a thin covering of salt over the skin.

Dressed drably like so many of the other peasant-farmers of Botswana, Morwakgosi wore an open-neck khaki shirt, dirty at the collar, and torn at the shoulder, while his long khaki trousers had been patched here and there with pieces of blue material. One leg of the trousers was torn at the knee; probably a vicious 'wait-a-bit' thorn tree had caught the trouser as he herded his cattle. On his feet he wore a pair of eland-skin sandals, very precious, soft and pliable, sewn carefully for him by an old, faithful Mokgalagadi servant of his. Only a man of some standing would wear such shoes. His soft felt hat, pushed back over his deeply wrinkled brow, had seen better days. The sand, blown by Kalahari winds, was

9

deeply ingrained in it, while the hole in front certainly gave a useful vent for fresh air.

THE CLOUDS OF WHITE DUST

Behind us, great clouds of white dust were thrown by the truck wheels into the still, hot air. The thorn bushes at the side of the road were white, dust-clad, and weary-looking, while in the distance a white haze hung over the thousands of mud huts of Molepolole, capital town of the Bakwena tribe of Botswana. The white haze was dust, dust that covered everything at the end of the long dry season; dust that was raised from the winding roads and pathways of the town; dust raised by people walking, by groups of happy naked children playing, by huge lumbering ox-wagons drawn through the town by teams of sixteen to twenty long-horned cattle, by herds of weary goats and oxen being taken for watering to the rapidly drying dams, and by the trucks which passed to and fro along the winding sandy ways.

Everything that moved raised clouds of fine dust into the azure sky. Only when the rains came would the dust settle, the sand be packed hard under lorry wheels, and the weary, resistant thorn scrub be washed to shine with fresh summer greenery.

This was the time of year when Molepolole was crowded with people, nearly 30,000 of them, living for the most part in picturesque round or rectangular, mud-walled, thatch-roofed houses. Almost 7,000 such buildings were, I was told by the young volunteers from Britain who helped with the census, spread out along a five-mile ridge of rock and shale. It was the time of year between harvest and the new plough-ing season. The crops had all been brought safely home from distant farms.

All through August and early September ox-wagons had lumbered home, creaking under their loads of sacks of millet, of great grass baskets filled with maize and beans, of pots and pans, of boxes and suitcases, of men, women, and children. All through the month of August the still, chilly nights had been disturbed by the shouts of men, cracking their long whips over the backs of weary oxen, and the rumble and creak of wheels told of ancient wagons home once more.

This was the time of year for repairing huts, for patching up yard walls washed away by thunder showers, for weddings and parties, for beer drinking, for settling disputes and quarrels, for attending church, for selling corn and buying dresses, sewing machines, radios, and bicycles. It was also the time of year when epidemics of measles and whooping cough swept through the crowded town, and old people died easily of pneumonia.

We passed the newly built secondary school on our left; a school built out of prefabricated materials, with laboratories and modern staff houses. It had just been built, with British money, to help meet the ever-growing problem of how to educate the many hundreds of young people clamouring for higher education. On our right stood the United Congregational church, a massive building, towering majestically over the surrounding huts. Morwakgosi told me how his father, with all the other able-bodied young men of the Tribe, had been sent by Chief Sechele II in 1907 to Johannesburg in order to work on the gold mines for the building of the church. I reminded him of how fifty years later Sechele's grandson, Kgari Sechele, had asked every man in the Tribe to give £1 for the enlarging of the original building. In the distance on our left we passed the Anglican church and then skirting round the government offices we found ourselves in a maze of huts.

Viewed from the air this mighty conglomeration of huts is not just a haphazard mass without form, as appears from the cab of a truck, but is a town with shape and pattern. The shape is roughly in great circles, with smaller circles of huts within the large circle. Each of the large circles represents a ward, or *kgotla* or a district. The smaller circles are *sub-kgotlas*, or sub-districts, or even just large family groups. Each district has its own hereditary headman and is divided up into numerous family groups. Some of the *kgotlas* are high in the social scale and are near the Chief's *kgotla*, which is called *Kgosing*; other *kgotlas* are small and of little importance in the social set-up. This lineage system is the foundation of Tswana life. Here in Molepolole, the paramount Chief Sechele is at the head, and under him are headmen and sub-headmen. Living near each head of a district are his brothers, cousins, and other relatives. It is said that each man in the Tribe knows his position in this lineage system which has been passed down through the generations.

We drove past Sechele's place, the *Kgosing*, which is the centre of tribal life, and then Morwakgosi directed me down a stony incline to his *kgotla*. Away to the north-west we could see, over the huts below us, across a wide valley to the vast rolling bushland of far Bakwena country. It stretched, this inhospitable land of thorn scrub, ninety miles to the north and almost 200 miles to the west and then continued beyond its man-made boundaries, as sandy grasslands, into the Bama-ngwato country to the north and to the waterless plains of the state lands of the Kalahari desert to the west.

AT HOME IN THE *KGOTLA*

Morwakgosi's *kgotla* was typical of a thousand others throughout the towns and villages of Botswana. There was a large circle of huts surrounding an open space, the village green; except that there was no greenery—only sandy soil out of which grew dried weeds with burrs and sticky, spiky seeds which clung to our socks when we dismounted from the truck. In the centre of the green was the cattle kraal, a circular enclosure made of dead tree-trunks sunk firmly in the ground. The entrance to this enclosure was closed securely at night, when the trek oxen and the milking cows had been brought home, by a thorn bush which, wedged firmly across the opening, made a door impenetrable by man or beast.

A couple of women were on their knees in the courtyard covering up the hard, sun-baked surface with a thin layer of moist earth and cattle dung. They used their hands to smear the mixture smoothly over the surface, the deft movement of their fingers making attractive designs as they worked. They wore their working clothes; skirts of coarse blue material, thick, heavy, and stiff; loose-fitting, mud-stained blouses, and squares of brightly coloured material on their heads. I noticed that one blouse was fastened with a large white thorn of a *moshu* tree, while the other woman's was fastened with a large safety-pin. They greeted us with broad smiles, sitting back from their kneeling position to pass the time of day with us.

We did not enter the main hut facing us. This was built by Morwakgosi for his wife. It was the main house of the three or four huts which made up the family group. It was certainly a hut of which Morwakgosi was justifiably proud. The door stood ajar, and inside I could see some modern furniture. I noted a high bed, the wooden feet of which were in empty canned fruit tins as a protection from white ants. In the centre were a polished table and four upright chairs. A vase of artificial flowers stood on the table. On the mud walls hung one or two pictures, a gaudy one of King Nebuchadnezzar eating grass with a horrible, insane expression on his face, and an enlarged, tinted photograph of Morwakgosi in an oval wooden frame, highly polished. There were shelves, cleverly moulded in the walls, holding such everyday utensils as cups and plates. Yes, Morwakgosi was wealthy and his wife had taste!

I noticed another hut, quite a small one, neatly constructed and perfectly thatched. It had two small windows and a low veranda all round, on which was sitting a girl of some twenty years of age. She wore a well-fitting, bright blue dress, and her curly springy hair was neatly tied in parallel rows by fine string. She looked clean, intelligent, and happy as she busily worked the sewing machine on the ground in front of her. The girl rose as we approached.

'This is my eldest daughter, Maria,' said Morwakgosi. 'The hut is hers. I built it for her last year.' Maria came forward and shook hands with me, slowly, gently, and shyly. She held out her right hand and placed her left palm on the right forearm. She was, as it was, welcoming me with two hands. She curtsied respectfully with head bowed and then, in the way of the older people, she grasped my thumb and shook it firmly.

The remaining hut was much inferior to the other two. It was low with no windows or veranda. The door was home-made out of strips of wood and the thatch looked as though it had just been thrown into position. On a goat-skin mat near the door lay a boy of some ten years of age, covered with layers of blankets. His pillow was home-made, out of a coarse material stuffed with bits of cloth. It was stony hard. His mother, tidily dressed in a long green dress, sat by his side. Her *duick* of bright blue material was pushed back on her head. Several other women sat near the child around the ashes of a small fire.

THE FEVERED BOY

The thatch was black with the smoke of many fires and thick with spider webs. Hens and chickens moved in and out through the open door, picking greedily at the grains of millet scattered here and there on the hut floor. The boy was fevered, restless, and breathing with great difficulty. It hardly needed the stethoscope's help to diagnose broncho-pneumonia.

'I'll take him to hospital,' I said to Morwakgosi.

He looked at his wife and said, 'Do you hear what the *lekgowa* (white man) says?'

'Yes,' said the boy's mother, 'he speaks well, let him take the child.'

The boy was taken out to the lorry and his mat placed for him on the back of the vehicle. With grunts and groans of 'my knees, my old back', his mother managed to climb up and sit alongside him.

'God will help him; we'll give him injections,' I shouted to Morwakgosi.

'God is good. He will help,' replied Morwakgosi.

If the child died he would say, 'Who can argue with God?' If the child lived he would say, 'God is good.' And that is what in due course he did say.

Back through dusty lanes between groups of huts. Happy children everywhere. There are certainly no unwanted children in Botswana. Many of these happy children would not know who their father was, but they were all assimilated into the family group. Here was true communal living. All shared the food together, food plentiful in years of good harvest and food scarce in time of drought.

We passed the 'Bakwena National Café', a small tin-roofed, brick-walled place where Mr. Mokone sold cigarettes, lemonade, cocacola, sweets, matches, bread, and biscuits. A group of youths stood idly by with gaudy shirts and hands thrust deep into drain-pipe trousers, youngsters who had been unable to find a place in the secondary schools and who were idling their lives away. A line of girls, walking one behind the other with buckets of water on their heads, passed by, and the boys shouted loudly after them. We came to the Camp, the government headquarters. The blue, black, and white Botswana flag hung limply in the still air. The little post office was crowded: the mail lorry which came three times a week from the Botswana capital of Gaberones had just arrived. Up the hill near the Chief's place a crowd of women were sitting on the ground, chatting happily among themselves. They were waiting for the mail. Soon Mr. Gasegale would come from the post office with a pile of letters. He would call out the name, written often with great difficulty by an illiterate man, on the envelope, and hand it to the woman concerned. With fast-beating heart she would open it, from her son or her husband working on the gold mines in far-off Johannesburg, and perhaps there would be a little money enclosed.

A whitewashed building near the post office had uneven lettering painted on its gable-end, 'H.M. Prison'. The letters had not yet been changed to 'Republic of Botswana, Prison'. A group of prisoners, in their khaki shorts, brown jerseys with a red stripe round the middle, sauntered by, laughing and joking with their guard, a young corporal, smart in his police uniform and very conscious of the well-known felt hat with one side turned up, of the Botswana constabulary.

'THE LAND IS GOOD'

The government offices looked clean and airy. The District Commissioner, a pleasant, efficient Motswana who had gradually over many years worked his way up in the civil service, could be seen hard at work at his desk. Independence had in no way lessened the amount of paper work! I noticed several clerks and some visitors moving leisurely from one office to another, the general office, the revenue office, the agricultural office, and the newly appointed famine-relief office. On the walls of the veterinary office, a separate building near the far end of the camp, were antelope horns mounted on wooden shields, kudu, eland, gemsbuk, springbuk, wildebeest, and hartebeest, giving a glimpse of the game to be seen in the western Kalahari.

Soon we passed the offices of the Witwatersrand Mine Recruiting Organization, from where twice a week scores of men are sent on the long journey to Johannesburg where they quickly adapt themselves to working at the pit-face 7,000 feet below ground. The recruiting agent was a white South African, sympathetic and helpful to his mine recruits, who respected him as a father. His house, with its wide gauzed-in veranda and green-painted roof, looked cool and peaceful, half hidden by the pepper, syringa, and jacaranda trees, just bursting out into early summer blossom. The flowering bushes which he had planted and watered so carefully, the oleanders, the pride of India, the hibiscus, and the poinsettias were in full bloom, showing off their brilliant colours, red, indigo, white, orange, and scarlet. The colours flashed in the drab brown landscape and seemed to cry with a loud voice saying, 'The land is good. Work the land, find water and this barren land will blossom as the rose!'

We stopped for a moment at one of the Indian stores near the recruiting office. The huge building of brick and corrugated iron was lined with shelves laden with blankets, cooking pots, tinned food, powdered milk, nuts and bolts, paint, cameras, radios, sugar, toilet requisites, and patent medicines. On the floor stood beds and furniture, pails and buckets, saddlery and radiograms. Anything could be bought, anything in fact that the progressive people of a newly independent Africa state would require. The shop was busy and the noise deafening as the cheery buyers shouted at each other and at Abdul and his Indian assistants. People were selling corn, some for cash and some for goods. If they took cash they were given six rands a bag, but if they took a little piece of paper on which was written 'goods-for' they could buy goods to the value of R7 in the shop. Naturally, the traders preferred to pay by 'goods-for'. They could sell off a lot of old stock by this means! The stores are great meeting-places and I noticed that many of the people were just standing chatting to each other, passing the hours away. School-children dressed in neat gym tunics had come to buy sugar, sweets, and tea.

The hospital gates came into view now. We had done a circular tour of Molepolole, a town typical of other towns and villages in Botswana, such as Serowe, capital of the Bamangwato tribe, Kanye, capital of the Bangwaketse, Mochudi, capital of the Bakgatla, Maun, capital of the Bata-wana, and Ramoutsa, capital of the Balete. I had spent a quarter of a century in this town of mud huts which gradually over the years, are giving place to brick and iron houses of modern design. I knew the town well, this town of a friendly, peaceful people whom I have served with all my strength and who in return have taught me much of patience, friend-ship, and endurance.

2

HOSPITAL IN THE DESERT

When you arrive you will probably say, as most people do, 'Oh! This is an oasis in the desert!' That, of course, is because you are dust-covered, hot, and tired, and you are gazing round at clean, cream-coloured buildings, with shady trees looking so cool in the brilliant sunshine.

The hospital, indeed, looks like a small village on the edge of Molepolole. The buildings are spread out over sixteen acres of ground and between them are trees of varying types and sizes, the tall blue gums, the shady peppers, the gentle jacarandas, and the hardy syringas, that tree found all over Botswana where the early missionaries settled, the only shady tree they could persuade to grow.

When I first went to Molepolole our source of water was one bore-hole about 200 feet deep which was fitted with a wind pump. When the wind blew, the pump worked and water was pumped into the one storage tank. Often, however, the wind did not blow, and so the tank was empty. We then had to rely on rain-water tanks placed at the corners of all the buildings. Towards the end of the dry season these were often empty, and so, if there was no wind, our water problems were acute!

Those waterless days are now almost gone. Only occasionally when pumps break, or after a very severe drought when the level of the water table falls very low, are we short of water. We now have three bore-holes, each about 300 feet deep. Each is fitted with a diesel pump, which means that we are not dependent on the wind for our supplies. Our third bore-hole was a gift from the Sunday School children of the United Free Church of Scotland. They sent us £1,000.

The art of finding funds is only learned slowly and painfully. I find that the thing to do is to state very clearly what you want and why, and then write to as many people and organizations as you think could possibly be interested. You keep on asking and you keep on praying. You must also keep very careful check on the funds you receive so that the donors see what you have done with their money. Every penny must be accounted for. This is time-consuming and requires great determination and perseverance. Soon after the end of the war, the United Free Church of Scotland had an extension scheme through which we were able to build a large operating theatre and staff houses. In 1949 we wired all the buildings and for the first time we had electric light supplied by our own two small generators. All this was done by funds raised by Scottish children through a 'Lamplighter Scheme'.

THE PATIENTS PAY

Most of our patients can afford to pay a small fee; most are willing to pay as much as they can afford if they feel they are to receive proper treatment. Nowadays, in Botswana, most mission and government hospitals make a charge of 4s. per visit. Some patients plead poverty, and we try various expedients to see if the poverty is genuine, as it can quite well be in times of drought or among old widows.

Pelonomi was a well-dressed young lady who entered the consulting-room saying, 'I am sorry, I have no money.'

I noticed that she was not seriously ill and that she was wearing a new dress. 'Oh, all right,' I said, 'just go outside and I'll see you when I've seen those who have brought their money.'

A willing nurse (who knew perfectly well that Pelonomi was trying us out) ushered Pelonomi outside. A few minutes later Pelonomi entered again, with the money in her hand. The nurse grinned and said, 'Well done, Doctor, she had the money all the time! She was trying to see how soft you would be!'

We also have the rich. Many come as private patients, making special appointments. They will travel many miles for this privilege and readily pay whatever fee is asked. These private patient fees certainly help the finances of the hospital. Several Tswana witch-doctors come regularly and usually produce a large roll of notes from the inside pocket of a tattered jacket. Nkale was one such. He banged down a five-pound note on the consulting-room table and demanded an injection costing that amount. This is quite a moral issue, as all he needed was an injection of penicillin costing a few shillings to cure his gonorrhoea. I usually compromise and charge him private patient fees and although he has not succeeded in losing his five-pound note he has paid something which marks him off as a little better than the ordinary patient and so he goes away quite satisfied!

NURSES IN TRAINING

We usually have about forty nurses in training. Those who have the Cambridge Junior Certificate study for the certificate offered by the Nursing Council of Lesotho, Botswana, and Swaziland, the three former High Commission Territories. Some of these nurses will be studying for the General Nursing Certificate, others for the Midwifery Certificate. Some will be first year and others second or third year. In addition, the hospital trains Enrolled Nurses, that is, girls who have not succeeded in obtaining the Junior Certificate, and who study for a nursing certificate offered by the Botswana government. These nurses play a great part in the nursing set-up of Botswana. The result is that the Sister Tutor finds herself with numerous small classes of students at varying levels and stages of training. Student nurses who obtain the certificate offered by the Nursing Council of Lesotho, Botswana, and Swaziland, are appointed staff nurses in government and mission hospitals, and, although their qualification is not reciprocal with the South African or British Nursing Council Certificates, they can be appointed ward sisters and several have been admitted into British hospitals for specialized studies.

The operating theatre is large by Botswana standards. It is green-painted, with tiles half-way up the walls. The equipment is modern, but not extravagant, sufficient to do all but highly specialized surgery. Much of the equipment has been donated by friends in Scotland and elsewhere, and many small plaques bearing names of people and organizations can be seen on the equipment. As you walk round the hospital, the impression gained is of cleanliness, efficiency, and happiness. The floors are spotless except at visiting hours, when sandy feet leave footmarks over the polished red cement! Sometimes people say, 'Fancy a mission hospital being so clean!' The beds are tidy with clean sheets, supplied by the women of the Church in Scotland. The blankets are red. These are not always appreciated. I told old Keokeditswe that I would admit her to hospital. 'Oh, no,' she replied, 'I am not going to sleep there, I fear those red blankets!'

This 16 acres of medical missionary endeavour is an oasis in the desert, a place of healing, of hope, of faith, and of prayer. For old Khumoyakgosi will be there morning and evening, taking prayers for staff and patients. All know that this is a place where, not only the body but the whole man, of mind and soul, is also healed. We are a big family, over 150 of us on the staff of this desert hospital, almost like a small town, all knowing each other. We quarrel, we disagree, we have our disciplinary problems and clashes of personalities, all of which are harder to deal with than the other innumerable, inanimate problems of leaking taps, blocked drains, cracked cylinder heads, scratched paint, and broken windows, and a thousand other daily snags and irritations. In spite of all this, we are a happy crowd of Africans and Europeans, proud of our buildings and equipment, proud of our medical and nursing standards, proud of the job we do with so few funds, proud to serve the friendly Bakwena people. This Scottish Livingstone Hospital of the United Free Church of Scotland is indeed an oasis in the desert of human need.

3

SIZING UP THE DOCTOR

To do any good in Africa a doctor has to win the full confidence of his patients. That confidence is won or lost in the out-patient department. It is here the people assess him and form their opinion of him—an opinion which is spread from mouth to mouth. The Batswana are intensely interested in medicine, in cures, in treatments, and especially in doctors whom they regard as almost having mystic powers.

Whenever a new doctor arrives, there is a temporary increase in the number of out-patients! They have come to see him, to test him, to form their opinion of him. The average Motswana is very wise and very accurate in assessing character. He is highly sensitive to attitudes of mind. He can tell at once whether the doctor is sympathetic to him or not. He does not look at the doctor's degrees, no matter how impressive they may be. He looks for patience, sympathy, and concern. If the doctor has these qualities, especially patience and concern, he will soon gain the confidence of the Batswana patients, who, when they trust him, will put themselves entirely in his hands for their treatment.

The new doctor is discussed in great detail: the shape and size of his ears and head; his mouth; the way he walks and swings his arms and holds his head; his figure, whether fat or thin; and above all, his skill or otherwise in dealing with people. Is he short-tempered or very patient? Is he proud and callous? Is he indifferent and unconcerned? Day by day the waiting crowds sit watching, listening, judging.

'Doctor, I have kidney trouble,' says the old man, placing his thumbs very dramatically and very accurately over the site of the kidneys.

'Doctor, I have womb trouble, I want an injection,' complains a young woman with gonorrhoea.

The new doctor tends to bristle at these remarks. 'Who told you it is your kidneys?' he might say to the old man. And the old man would think him very ignorant for does not everyone know where the kidneys are? Gradually the doctor learns to forget his pride and patiently to enter into the thought life of his patients.

'I HAVE COME FOR AN INJECTION'

The daily clinics show a lively picture of the variety and types of people living in Botswana today. They also show the wide variety of disease which still abounds. The educated government servant is always there. For him treatment is free; that is one of the terms of contract. He comes, well-dressed, smart suit, and speaks excellent English. Sometimes his symptoms have been carefully written down on a piece of paper which is handed to the doctor for his perusal. He is highly sensitive to the doctor's attitude to him. He wants a careful examination.

This educated, well-dressed government official may be followed into the consulting-room by an elderly woman, simply dressed in blouse and long blue skirts. Her face is lined, her teeth loose and decayed, her nails long and dirty, her body unwashed. 'I have come for an injection,' she says. That is all she wants; she is convinced that an injection of a vitamin or an antibiotic will drive away the pains of old age.

The old lady is followed by a young woman with two children, whose faces are clean and shining, and whose pretty dresses are new and clean. When we lift up the dresses for examination we find the little bodies still covered with yesterday's white dust from play. The dresses had been quickly put on out of respect for the doctor.

Another woman comes straight from work at the fields. A ragged square of material is on her tousled head her blouse is torn and dirty, her skirt shabby and dirty. A baby, naked except for a string of beads round its waist, is at the breast. She is followed by a clerk's wife with baby. She is a young educated woman, fashionably dressed and her expensive underclothing is spotlessly clean. In her excellent English she talks of the illness of her baby. Proudly she shows her baby, nicely dressed, well powdered, and wearing rubber pants over the nappy. In its mouth is a dummy, a sure sign of civilization!

'My blood is going all over my body,' complains a young woman with muscular rheumatism.

'The womb is rising up and going to my head,' complains an elderly woman with high blood pressure.

Constipation is complained of almost universally, but it is a very relative term. The doctor who prescribes a strong purgative is sure to be popular. All our patients bring their own bottles, usually empty lemonade or brandy bottles, and they consider their treatment incomplete if they do not go away with a bottle of drinking medicine, some pills, a little ointment, and, if they can persuade the doctor, an injection. They all expect the stethoscope to be used, even although the disease may only be a sore toe!

THE CORKSCREW-SHAPED GERM

Endemic syphilis, an unusual and interesting disease, used to be extremely common, but its incidence is now low, except perhaps in distant Kalahari villages and among the Bushmen. This is a type of syphilis affecting children, non-sexual in spread and not hereditary in origin.

One day a woman came with two children aged five and three, and a baby at the breast. 'We are all suffering from syphilis,' she said. Each child showed the raised, white, oozing patches of syphilis in the mouth and around the groins. The baby with these highly infectious sore in the mouth, was sucking at the breast, on which, near the nipple, was a similar syphilitic sore. The mother had been infected from the baby, who in turn had been infected from the other children. All the children were highly infectious and the disease would pass readily to other children who played or ate with them. An injection of penicillin rendered each child non-infectious and hastened the disappearance of the sores, but blood examination revealed that the whole body had been invaded by the corkscrew-shaped germ of syphilis.

The great danger of this endemic syphilis is that, if not thoroughly treated, it can, in the future, cause the destructive lesions of tertiary syphilis. In 1956 I conducted a mass treatment campaign against endemic syphilis throughout the whole country. In some Kalahari villages we found that 70 per cent of the inhabitants had been infected at one time with endemic syphilis. We wondered if, by ridding the country of endemic syphilis which conferred immunity, we would find at a later stage that venereal syphilis would increase in incidence. It seems that this is now happening as we find daily, at the out-patient clinics, cases of classical venereal syphilis. These cases, together with the very common venereal disease, gonorrhoea, are very numerous. These diseases can be rapidly cured with modern antibiotics, but the moral problem remains and grows more acute.

Puso brought his attractive young wife to me one day. Both looked glum. 'We want a child,' he said. 'I married this girl some six months ago and still she is not pregnant. I want to go to the mines to work and I want to know that she is pregnant before I go.' I put Puso out while I examined his wife.

'Has he started to scold you yet?' I asked the downcast-looking girl. I well knew what her reply would be.

'Oh yes. And now he has begun to beat me, saying I am a useless wife and that soon he will send me back home to my mother and he will find another wife for himself.'

When I examined her I found she had gonorrhoea, probably contracted from her husband. Most likely her 'tubes' were blocked and inflamed with the infection. I called Puso in and explained first of all that he should not be so impatient; after all, six months was not a long time to wait for a child; and I also said that he and his wife would be given a course of injections. That pleased him greatly. They were both given a course of penicillin injections and after another six months Puso went happily off to the mines and his wife regularly attended the ante-natal clinic.

'I NEED A CHILD IN MY OLD AGE'

Sterility and infertility are dreadful things for an African woman. A husband likes his wife to become pregnant im-

25

mediately after marriage. She is then a proper, dutiful, respected wife. That is what, in addition to cooking his food and looking after the crops, every husband expects of his wife. When she fails in this duty her life becomes a misery; she is despised by her husband and pitied by her relatives and friends. The blame for lack of children is always placed on the wife, although it is now known that often the cause lies with the husband. We usually take these unhappy women into hospital for full investigation and treatment, and frequently we are able to help them. If all our efforts fail, the husband often divorces her, or goes secretly to other women to raise children by them and so prove his potency.

Even women who have despaired of marriage come asking for treatment for sterility. 'How can you have a child when you are not married?' I asked Anna, who had come in her late thirties begging for a child.

'I need a child in my old age and there is never a shortage of men,' was her reply.

Many of these infertile women wander from hospital to hospital throughout the country, hoping against hope that some doctor, somewhere, will be able to help.

Most women want large families. Wapula came into the consulting-room one day. 'I want children,' she said imploringly. 'I am so anxious to have children.'

'How many have you now?' I asked.

'Only four alive and six have gone to Heaven,' she replied, pointing upwards to the ceiling.

'Then surely you must be satisfied, and in any case you are over forty now, Wapula,' I suggested.

'No, indeed, I am not satisfied. I want more and, as regards my age, please note that my friends of the same age are still having children.' She was rather hurt.

On a subsistence economy, of course, children are an asset: the more hands, the more farming can be done. And when the infant mortality rate is so high it is always a good idea to have a few extra children around.

The first child, especially if a girl, is often given to the grandmother to help her in her old age, and other children may be given to childless relatives. Boys are needed for herding cattle and girls for carrying water and working in the fields. Changes are, however, taking place and many of the educated Batswana are content with four children. We find many women asking about family planning. Those who have had numerous children are usually sterilized a day or two after childbirth in hospital. Other women are given the 'pill', but for most we find the intra-uterine device the best answer.

THE MENTALLY ILL

Some of the most depressing cases brought to the daily clinics are the mentally ill people. Dikeledi was aged about twenty. She had been 'unconscious' since fighting with her husband, who now thought that she was near to death. Some six strong men lifted her down from the wagon that had brought her from her farm. She lay as if in deep coma. She would not speak or respond to any stimulus. Pins were stuck in her limbs without any response. It took several days in hospital before the hysteria passed from her and she was well enough for a distraught husband to take her home. She had certainly given him a fright and had taught him a salutary lesson!

Mental cases seem to find a peculiar satisfaction in attending church and interrupting the services. For years we had one old lady who was a most regular attender. Everyone was afraid of her as she walked down the aisle with a wicked grin on her face and a great bundle on her head. She would set herself down on the floor, and muttering to herself would undo the huge bundle, displaying rags, bicycle pumps, cooking pots, and numerous other articles for all to see. As soon as the sermon started she would stand up and at the top of her voice argue with the preacher. Once or twice we descended on her, bundled her into a van and drove rapidly to the far end of the village, from where, if she decided to walk back to church, she would find that even a long-winded preacher would have drawn his sermon to a peaceful conclusion!

The missionary doctor in the area is also the district surgeon and so is involved in a good deal of medico-legal work, a work which is increasing as the years go by. There has been quite a rise in the number of assault cases and, especially at the week-ends, people with bleeding heads or stab wounds are brought regularly to the hospital. The number of assault cases is, however, still far less than the number found in the big cities of South Africa, and most are not very severe. Brutal murder does occur, usually due to sudden anger in a drunken brawl or to deep jealousy. Jealousy between wives of polygamists or between 'girl-friends' and wives has resulted in a number of serious assaults and murders. Ritual murder cases also occur and the Independent government is doing all in its power to stamp out this evil superstition. Women fight with their teeth, and frequently we have a piece of ear or the end of a finger brought with the request that it be sewn back on; unfortunately, apart from leopard bites, I know of no wound which so readily becomes infected as a human bite!

Twice a week we examine recruits for the gold mines of Johannesburg and the platinum and asbestos mines of the western Transvaal. There may be up to 150 men to examine at a time, and for this service we receive 2s. 6d. per man for the first 500 in a year and then 1s. per man. For such a sum, and with such large numbers of men, only a rather cursory examination is expected of us by the mining companies. The main aim is to weed out men with obvious diseases, such as tuberculosis, deformities, blindness, deafness, and other conditions which would make them useless for heavy work underground. A number of the men have been to the witch-doctor beforehand to be given medicine which makes sure that they pass the medical examination! There are usually a few men with lash marks down their backs. They have recently been thrashed by their fathers, or in their *kgotla*, and they are going off to work to get away from it all. Each man breathes deeply as his chest is examined and the clerk turns his head to one side as halitosis due to pyorrhoea is often quite marked. These young men can go either on a four-month or a nine-month contract. In a year of drought some 5,000 from the Bakwena area alone, will seek work at the mines, where they are well cared for.

It is the ambition of every herd-boy, when he reaches the age of seventeen years to go to the mines. If their fathers will not allow them to go, these young men often run away and recruit themselves without their fathers' knowledge. Some are sent to work to earn money for their father or master. Most go because they want to earn money and because they like the adventure and the work in the white man's city. In the awful drought years of 1962 to 1966, thousands of men from all over Botswana flocked to Johannesburg, and the money they sent home enabled wives and mothers to buy food for their families. Botswana needs employment for her men and she needs money; South Africa needs the labour force, and so both countries are happy with this arrangement.

Sitting in the out-patient consulting-room year by year, one comes to know, to admire and to love the Batswana. I came to Botswana to heal and to teach and to give. I find that I also learn and receive. I learn patience and I see how to endure and how to accept submissively all the problems and tragedies of life. I receive affection and trust. I see eyes turned to me for help, and in those needy eyes of the Bakwena I see the eyes of Christ, and I know that as I serve them I serve him who said, 'Inasmuch as you have done it unto one of the least of these my brethren you have done it to me.'

4

WHERE THE LION AND THE LEOPARD PROWL

Very often a ward round in our desert hospital is like going through a textbook of medicine. The patient arrives, you examine him, you X-ray him yourself, you do any laboratory test you can with your limited equipment, you make your diagnosis, you decide whether to operate, you operate if you think necessary and the patient agrees, you anaesthetize the patient, you deal with the disease at operation, you find a blood donor if possible and if needed, you type the blood and cross-match it with the patient's, you put up the transfusion. You watch your case from beginning to end. If there are two of you, or, better still, three, the strain is not so great. Being an ordained minister I sometimes have to bury my patient at the end!

LEOPARD IN THE TRAP

The surgical ward has always a variety of cases, some sel-dom seen in hospitals in more developed parts of the world. Madimabe was an old man from a Kalahari village some sixty miles to the west of Molepolole. His wizened, deeply lined face was adorned with a scraggy, white, goat-like beard, and his eyes always twinkled when he spoke. He was extremely rich in cattle and also he was a renowned hunter. He special-ized in leopard hunting because the price he could obtain for a leopard skin far exceeded the price for any other type of skin, including lion. He usually hunted on horseback, with a pack of lean, hungry dogs.

Deep in the Kalahari bush he would find the 'spoor' or footprints of a leopard. With sharp eyes which could read the signs on the veld as an educated man would read a book, he would follow the footmarks of the animal until he and his dogs came across it, crouching beneath a bush or lying on a tree branch. The barking, snapping dogs would keep the leopard at bay while old Madimabe would shoot it with his ancient and highly inaccurate rifle, from the saddle. The leopard which brought him to hospital, however, was caught in a trap.

The old man had set a vicious, steel trap with jagged teeth, hoping to catch a springbok or hare. Instead, he caught a leopard which had inadvertently placed its paw on the trap, causing the teeth to spring together over its paw with a grip that could not be loosened. The trap was tied by a piece of rope to a stake driven firmly into the ground. When Madimabe came to see what he had caught he found a furious leopard, wild with agony, leaping, growling, and snarling in a most frightening way. Madimabe advanced on foot to shoot the leopard at close quarters. The shot was fatal; but before the agonized creature died, it made one last desperate effort to free itself. The stake was pulled out of the ground and the dying beast, with the cruel trap still on its paw, hurled itself, a ball of fury, with claws outstretched and teeth bared, upon the old man.

They rolled over and over on the ground, the animal trying with all its dying strength to tear Madimabe's throat out, while the hunter pushed with all his strength at the beast's face. In a few moments the leopard lay dead across Madimabe's chest. He pushed the animal from him and staggered to his feet with blood pouring from deep gashes in his head, shoulders, and hands. Next day a passing lorry brought him to hospital. Sepsis, so inevitable with leopard wounds, had set in; pus and serum oozed from the deep wounds and a high fever raged. In spite of large doses of antibiotics abscesses formed over the next few months, and the fever continued for many days. Eventually he recovered and returned to his Kalahari village, where, dressed in old shirt and buckskin trousers he spent his declining years instructing younger men how to hunt leopards.

A LION'S MAUL

We often remember our Bushman with lion wounds. He was brought to us one cold winter's morning just as the red sun was peeping above the distant hills. The man who spoke to me was a rosy-faced young British constable, dressed in the uniform of the Bechuanaland Protectorate Police. 'Sorry to trouble you, Doc, but I have brought a Bushman mauled by a lion.' I walked up to the hospital with him, shivering in the early morning cold. The grass in places was white with overnight frost. The Chevrolet police truck was standing at the hospital entrance. Like all vehicles which travel in the Kalahari it was heavily laden: petrol and water drums, bedding rolls, food boxes, passengers, and a couple of smart Batswana policemen. Right at the tail of the lorry was a dead springbok, lying grotesquely on top of a large bundle of blankets. On removing the springbok we discovered that in the bundle was a tiny, elderly, scraggy Bushman, almost frozen stiff, with huge foul-smelling wounds in his shoulders and buttocks. On closer examination we saw that most of the right buttock had been torn away and that the deep shoulder wounds extended as huge scratch marks down his back.

'What happened, Sarge?' I asked.

'We found him about two hundred miles west, near a little Makgalagadi village,' replied the sergeant, wiping a drip off his cold nose with his gloved hand. He had cause to be cold as he had driven all through the frosty Kalahari night. 'It seems that he had been out hunting for hares, when he disturbed a lioness with cubs. She sprang on him and threw him in the air as a cat would a mouse. She mauled him and then sat back to watch him. He had the presence of mind to feign death, lying perfectly still as blood oozed from his wounds. After a while the lioness walked away and the Bushman dragged himself to the Makgalagadi village, where, fortunately for him, he was found by our patrol the next day.'

We dressed his wounds, pulling what flaps of tissue were still viable together with large sutures. A clean white gown, white sheets, red blankets, and a high hospital bed did not relieve his obvious terror of his new abode! Hospitalization with its smells of antiseptic, its doctors and nurses in white, was quite outside his experience and was a greater trial to him than the lion wounds. He soon removed himself from the bed, discarded his nightgown, untied the bandages, and, but for the timely arrival of a nurse, would have taken out the stitches. For a day or two he was delirious, but large doses of antibiotics and sedatives did their work, and eventually he was persuaded to wear a nightgown and to leave the bandages alone. After a few days a local man who knew Sesarwa, his language, helped us to converse with him.

The first thing the Bushman said was, 'Where are the two little children I left tied up in a tree?' It is Bushman practice, when out on a dangerous hunt, to leave tiny children, who might wander away, tied up in trees, from the safety of which they are retrieved when the hunt is over. We contacted the willing sergeant, who once again set off on his 200-mile journey back to find the missing children. On reaching the village he was informed that the children were quite safe, having been found by other Bushmen.

Several plastic operations were required to restore the Bushman's torn flesh and he seemed to settle down in hospital and was a great favourite with the nurses, although we sensed that he was not really at home with us. When he was well enough to walk about the wards, he asked to be discharged, pointing avidly to the far west. The recruiting agent for the gold-mining companies promised to return him to the village where he had been found, on his next monthly trip into the Kalahari.

The first night out, some 120 miles west of Molepolole, camp was made and the recruiting agent with his men slept round a large camp-fire. The Bushman rolled himself in his thin blanket and lay close to the fire. In the early morning, while still dark, he slipped quietly away into the great Kalahari desert, limping into the waterless bush, wandering away home in the great thirsty land. We saw him no more.

SOLOMON AND THE SNAKE

Snakes are numerous around the hospital buildings and in the bush around Molepolole; cobras, rattle snakes, green and black mambas and pythons are all seen regularly. In spite of that only a small number of cases of snake-bite are admitted each year to hospital.

Solomon, a thin child of some eight years, was bitten by a black mamba on his finger, while looking for honey in a rocky outcrop of limestone. He arrived at the hospital gate a few days later on a cattle-drawn sledge. His fingers and hand became gangrenous and only an operation through the forearm saved his life. Amputation is the only operation, nowadays, to which the Bakwena strenuously object, and many a case of skin and bone cancer has gone home to die rather than face a mutilating operation.

Solomon's father, seeing the foul-smelling gangrene spreading slowly up his child's arm reluctantly agreed to the operation. Father knew that Solomon's future would be hard. He will not bother to send him to school, and when his comrades in their late teens go off to the gold mines he will have to stay behind with the cattle. He will be nicknamed 'rra-sekweni' the 'one-handed one', and his life will be spent at a far distant cattle post. Like the deformed, the maimed, the disfigured, the blind and deaf of Botswana, he will be kept hidden away at distant farms until, perhaps as development proceeds, schools and homes will be opened for such people.

There is only one surgical condition which is, I think, peculiar to Africans, although it is possible that it might be found in other races who go continually bare-footed. Lerato had always gone barefooted for her seventy-odd years of life. In hospital she always sat up in bed with the red blankets tucked tightly under her chin. She talked incessantly to the other patients, and each day she showed me her toes, begging for something to be done. The small toe of each foot looked as though a piece of string had been tied tightly round its base and was gradually separating the toe from the foot. This condition is called 'Ainhum' and the cause is not known. Eventually, after much suffering, the fifth toe drops off. We lessened Lerato's period of suffering by removing the toes under a local anaesthetic. In a day or two she hobbled down the road with a grateful smile on her old face. A year later she brought half a bag of corn to the hospital to show her intense gratitude.

There are always eye cases in the surgical wards. Trachoma,

34

a virus infection of the conjunctivae, is common, especially in the dry Kalahari areas. As the disease burns itself out, the eyelids contract with scar tissue and turn inwards, with a result that the eyelashes rub on the sensitive cornea. This causes ulceration and eventual blindness. A fairly simple operation to turn the eyelids outwards gives a measure of comfort and saves the eye. Cataract in the elderly is commonly seen. We used to tackle these cases ourselves with varying degrees of success, but now that Dr. Teichler, a missionary doctor of the Dutch Reformed Church at Mochudi, has specialized in eye work we send most of our cases to him, some sixty miles away.

INTO THE FIRE

Epilepsy is remarkably common in Botswana, and relatives are often very careless in guarding epileptics from fire danger.

Kgole had been in and out of hospital several times with deep burns, but his latest burns were the most extensive he had yet had. He was sitting round a huge fire with his family one cold night when he was thrown into the fire with his epilepsy. He was brought on a sledge to the Letlhakeng clinic after a few days. The upper part of his body had escaped injury but the lower part was a mass of deep, infected burns. He managed to walk from the sledge to the clinic with a blanket thrown over his shoulders. He was taken to Molepolole and nursed on the gauzed-in veranda, where such cases are often nursed. The stench of rotting flesh, however, pervaded the whole hospital, so that patients were unable to eat their food and those who were allowed out of bed spent all their time out of doors. We finally erected a small prefabricated round hut in which Kgole was nursed. His courage and endurance were wonderful to see, and eventually after numerous skin-grafting operations, he recovered.

Bogadi was a similar case. He lay for several minutes with his legs in a roaring fire. It was four days later before he reached hospital, where his gangrenous legs were amputated above the knees in order to save his life. He has now fastened pieces of old car tyre round the stumps and crawls around on these.

It is easy for an infant sleeping close to the fire to roll over in its sleep and land up in the flames. Dikeledi brought her nine-month-old baby, quite badly burned.

'People put him in the fire in the middle of the night,' she said.

'You mean, baloi? (witches)' I asked.

'Yes, indeed,' replied Dikeledi.

'You should not blame witches for your own carelessness,' I rejoined. 'You know you should not have let your baby sleep so close to the fire.'

Two diseases of the Western world, however, have rarely, if ever, been seen in our wards. One is multiple sclerosis, the dreaded 'creeping paralysis' of colder climates, and the other is that great killer of the white races, coronary thrombosis. Multiple sclerosis has never been diagnosed in Botswana, and I believe it is extremely rare among all races who were born in the Republic of South Africa. On the other hand, coronary thrombosis is exceedingly common among the white business and professional men in South Africa. I have only seen two or three cases of this disease among the Batswana, proved by the electrocardiogram, since I came to Botswana. That is three cases in twenty-five years. Yet among the small white population of Botswana I have seen a dozen or so cases in the last few years. Perhaps the average white person eats too much rich food, smokes too many cigarettes, worries continuously, rushes around on his business too much, and exercises himself too little.

The average Motswana eats simple food with a low fat content, smokes few cigarettes, takes his time about his daily activities, worries little over his finances, although he does worry over his cattle, knows nothing of the fluctuations of the stock market, and above all from youth to old age he walks continuously. He walks many miles herding cattle, he walks from his home to his cattle post and lands. When at home he walks to the shops, to church, and to the chief's kgotla. His coronary arteries do not have a chance to become blocked; the constant gentle exercise keeps them well open.

It always puzzles me why, when coronary heart disease is so rare, high blood pressure should be so common. Many educated Batswana suffer from this disease, which is characteristically associated with the same causes as coronary heart disease. The more we search for this condition the more cases we find. Many cases are related to the commonly found kidney infections, but other cases are similar to the 'essential hypertension' of the European, with no obvious cause found.

A strange and disappearing disease is *onyalai*. Boineelo had several attacks during her life. She came into hospital with severe bleeding from the nose and gums. Inside her mouth were numerous large, black, 'blood blisters', medically known as bullae. She also had large bruises in her thighs and numerous tiny red spots were scattered over her body. This disease is very similar to the purpura of white people and is caused by a lack of platelets in the blood. It used to be common among the African people of Rhodesia and the Republic of South Africa, but all reports suggest that it is seen much less now than previously. No one knows the cause, and we see fewer cases today than we did twenty years ago. Perhaps improved diet and living conditions are a factor in its disappearance.

BABIES—DYING AND LIVING

The infant mortality rate in Botswana is not known because statistics are not regularly kept, but it must be quite high. Most women who have had seven or more children report that three or four of them have died in infancy. We used to admit our child patients to the verandas, but now that a fine spacious children's ward has been opened we can offer the sick children much better medical services.

One of the problems is that mothers usually breast-feed their babies until they are around eighteen months old, and such a mother is loath to let her baby suddenly leave the breast for admission to hospital. The result is that frequently when we admit a baby we admit the mother as well. Modern child psychologists would no doubt support us in this, but it can be a difficult psychological exercise when beds are scarce.

The opposite also holds true: when we admit a mother we often find there is a baby to be admitted as well.

Little Peter was sixteen months old but he looked as though he was six months. His wiry, curly hair was straight and ginger-coloured. The spring and life had gone out of it. His face was pinched and wrinkled but his tummy was swollen, due to an enlarged liver. His legs were swollen, due to fluid accumulating in the tissues, and the skin was dry and cracked, giving it the appearance of 'crazy paving'. He had diarrhoea, no appetite, and lay still and listless. He was a case of kwashiorkor, a disease found throughout Africa in children recently weaned, and due to protein and vitamin deficiency. This is a serious disease with a high death rate.

Peter was given an intravenous infusion and a diet of a special protein powder and vitamins. Gradually his hair regained its black colour and spring, and the swollen liver and legs returned to normal. Peter regained an interest in life and played all day with a teddy bear sent to the hospital from friends in Scotland. This teddy bear had come before Christmas along with numerous other toys from women's associations of the United Free Church of Scotland. When Peter was discharged he was given a bottle of concentrated orange juice, a supply of vitamin tablets, and his mother was advised about his diet. She shrugged her shoulders, smiled and said, 'I hear.' It was a year of drought, with milk and protein food scarce and expensive. Peter went home to his maize-meal diet and when his symptoms returned his mother did not bother to bring him back to the hospital. She just sat and watched him die.

In the cot next to Peter's was Pelonomi, a little Mokgalagadi girl from Motokwe, 180 miles west of Molepolole. She was an attractive, shy little girl, pretty, except that her scalp was covered with a thick white crust which was cracked in places to reveal a red tender skull beneath. When she arrived the whole scalp was a mass of flies, so persistent in their efforts to feed upon the diseased skin that Pelonomi had long since despaired of ever driving them away, and so she left them to feed untroubled. This disease, which is found mainly among the children in the Kalahari desert areas where standards of hygiene are poor, is known by the Afrikaans name of *witkop* meaning 'whitehead'. The Setswana name for this disease is *digwaba*. We used to think that this disease was one of the manifestations of endemic syphilis but now know that it is caused by a type of fungus and its medical name is *favus*. When the disease is eventually healed the scalp is left permanently bald as the hair follicles are destroyed. Treatment is long and difficult in spite of the use of new anti-fungal drugs and oitments. Soap and water used regularly would prevent the spread of this disease, and I have no doubt that before long, as the standard of hygiene rises in the Kalahari villages, this disease, like endemic syphilis, will be seen no more.

Young Tetlo had suffered a great deal before he was brought to hospital. A few weeks previously he had developed severe pain and swelling in the thigh. The affected thigh became hot, swollen, tender. Tetlo suffered stoically for many days until at last one day the abscess which had commenced in the femur bone burst through the skin. Day after day large quantities of pus drained from the wound. Tetlo lay for several weeks in his dark hut, becoming ever more emaciated and weak. At last a trader's lorry brought him to hospital. X-rays showed pieces of dead bone lying deep in the femur. At operation these pieces were removed and Tetlo rapidly recovered, and soon, with a slight limp, went back to his cattle.

As soon as the children are well enough, they are allowed to play with the toys so liberally sent from overseas. If they are lucky enough to be in hospital at Christmas they are given a doll or a toy truck to take home. The joy of an eight-year-old girl receiving a doll for the first time in her life has to be seen to be believed. And how proud she is when she takes it home, even although she knows that her older sisters will take it from her and claim it as their own! Especially do the children love the swing so kindly donated by Mrs. Sechele, widow of Chief Kgari Sechele. Indeed, hospital for the little ones, when recovery is taking place, is a thrilling and exciting place of new experiences and pleasures, a peep indeed into the world of white people! On Sundays, they have a Sunday

School where they sing choruses in their sweet voices, clapping their hands:

> *Wide, wide, as the ocean,*
> *High as the Heaven above,*
> *Deep, deep, as the deepest sea*
> *Is my Saviour's love.*

Then they are told a Bible story, and sometimes one of them may hear for the first time of the great love of God for little children. Most, however, have already heard the gospel story at home or at school, and all have a deep faith and trust in a great God who controls wind and rain, hunger and plenty, life and death.

And on a Sunday evening the adult patients gather together with their hymn books, and in their appealing, plaintive voices sing hymns and praises to God. Then we thank God for our calling, to heal his children and tell them of his love, and we thank him that he uses such as us in the work of making people whole.

5

FIVE MILES FOR THE BABY

I had only been a few days in Molepolole when my first abnormal maternity case arrived. All day she had travelled on the bumpy ox wagon through sand and over rough stones, drawn by twelve weary oxen. An old mattress, covered with goat-skin mats had been placed in the centre of the wagon, and on this, with her mother squatting by her side, Bonang had lain, groaning occasionally as the tired womb made ineffective efforts to expel the unborn child. Several of Bonang's aunts and a grandmother were also sitting on the lumbering wagon, their faces anxious, muttering to each other that witchcraft was preventing the birth of the child. Her husband drove the oxen hard, lashing out mercilessly with his long whip and yelling loudly at the struggling oxen to stir them on to greater efforts. It was ten o'clock at night before the lights of the hospital came into view and the wagon creaked its way through the west gate. Bonang's husband, weary and dust-covered, blurted out, 'The child refuses to be born.' Then he walked away, leaving the old women to give greater details. The wizened old grandmother did most of the talking, inhaling snuff from the palm of her hand as she spoke.

'She has been more than two days in labour; the child is lying wrongly. The Setswana doctor says the fault is her paternal grandmother's, whose heart is sore and bitter after quarrelling with Bonang's husband.'

Bonang was indeed ill. She was cold, clammy, and foul-smelling. One glance gave me the diagnosis.

'Oh dear,' I groaned, 'an impacted shoulder presentation and it is her first pregnancy!' Protruding out of her was a baby's arm, swollen and blue, with decaying skin peeling off, over gas-filled blisters. Her lower abdomen was swollen like a balloon.

The baby had long since died in the womb. I had no alternative but to perform a destructive operation and remove the putrefying child in pieces. Bonang made a satisfactory recovery, and, although I had only arrived in the country, I realized that a paramount need was for a properly conducted ante-natal clinic. This was, at that time, an unheard-of thing, and it was quite exceptional for the old women to bring their daughters to hospital for confinement. This, I realized, was pioneer ground, and the possibilities of helping here had to be explored.

When Bonang left the hospital I warned her and her relatives that she had a contracted pelvis and that 'should God again bless her with a pregnancy' she must report at once for examination. After eighteen months she appeared again and I felt that with her, as an example of what could be done, our ante-natal clinic would prosper. When her labour pains commenced she reported at once to the hospital. We did our first ever Caesarean section and gave Bonang a healthy baby girl. Her relatives were thrilled and the fame of our hospital spread. The operation was the talk of the town.

Then tragedy struck! A few days after the operation, a clot of blood dislodged itself from a vein in the pelvis, travelled silently through the heart to lodge in the lungs. Bonang gave a gasp of pain, struggled for breath and then died. I wondered if we would ever again be allowed to do a Caesarean section, for Bonang's parents had taken a good deal of convincing about the value of such an operation, and I knew that news of our failure would now be the talk of the town. Gradually, however, confidence was won, and today if a Caesarean operation is necessary we just do it and tell the relatives afterwards!

RACE AGAINST DEATH

The pressing need for ante-natal care was soon brought home to me in other vivid ways. I remember one Sunday evening at harvest time. Two men arrived on bicycles at sunset. They had obviously travelled far, as they were dust-covered and tired. The senior man spoke. 'We left our lands when the sun was straight overhead and we have travelled as fast as the sand would allow. There is a young woman in labour pains. The women say she cannot deliver herself. Will the doctor please come to help her?'

I changed out of my Sunday suit into khaki shirt and trousers. I put an obstetrical bag and a stretcher on to the Bedford truck, took a torch and pressure lamp, collected a staff nurse and set off for the distant farm with one of the two men in the cab to guide us through the winding bush roads. The journey took us along a wagon track between thick thorn scrub which tore viciously at the sides of the truck, while sharp stumps of trees, hidden in the sand, jagged at the tyres. Presently we passed fields of ripening corn and numerous groups of huts at which contented people were sitting round evening fires, chatting quietly together.

After a couple of hours driving the guide said, 'We are nearly there.' The nurse said, 'It is still a long way, Doctor.' I decided to believe the nurse and settled down for another hour's drive. We drove on and on through thick scrub where only a narrow footpath showed the way. Spring hares, with eyes flashing like torches, hopped across our path, and now and again a duiker or a jackal jumped across the path. At last the guide said, 'We have arrived.' That was a euphemistic understatement, about which he and the staff nurse entered into an acrimonious argument. After half an hour the huts came into view. They were on the edge of a large field of ripe millet. A few old men were sitting huddled together with half a dozen small naked children round a fire. They greeted us politely as we made our way round to the miserable hut at the back, the entrance to which was closed with a thorn bush.

We called the Tswana words used when entering a house, 'Ko, ko.' The thorn bush was pulled aside and we entered a small hut filled with acrid smoke from a small fire burning on the floor. The smoke brought tears to our eyes, tears which became real when we saw our patient. She was sitting with her back against the mud wall of the hut. On either side of her crouched an old woman who appeared to be taking turns at massaging her abdomen. Another old woman crouched in front of her, ready it seemed to catch the unborn

43

babe. I flashed the torch to see better in the flickering light. I saw a baby's head just showing and I saw the great swelling of a distended bladder. Quickly I pushed the old woman aside and crouched where she had been, in front of the young woman. I shone my torch directly on to her face and saw an attractive girl of some twenty years of age. The eyes were glazed, the pupils made no response to the flash of the torch. Even before I put my stethoscope to her chest I knew that she was dead; dead with the child that had killed her still inside, dead after days of suffering; dead unnecessarily; two lives lost through ignorance, lives which could have been saved.

'She's gone,' I said to the old women, as I groped my way unsteadily to the door. The old women threw themselves on the ground, wailing piteously.

TONIC AND TABLETS

'Every woman who is pregnant should come for examination.'

'When you are in your last month of pregnancy do not stay far away at the lands, rather come home and stay near the hospital.'

'When the labour pains start, walk at once to the hospital.'

We preach this three-fold message every week at the clinic and then we say, 'Go and tell other women what you have heard.' The battle is more or less won now. The Bakwena women in large numbers attend the ante-natal clinic and watch with quiet interest as they are weighed, their blood taken for examination, and their blood pressures recorded. They love the thorough examination given them by student nurses and trained staff. Then they walk away with a bottle of iron tonic balanced on their heads and a supply of vitamin tablets in their hand.

In 1948 I told the women of the United Free Church of Scotland of our great need for a maternity ward. One day a lady gave me a cheque for £1,000 to start our fund. This was in the days before the big charitable organizations such as Oxfam were offering to help, and I was absolutely thrilled. In a short time the ladies of the church raised another £2,000 and we built our first ten-bedded maternity block. Thanks to recent help from Oxfam and 'Bread for the World' of Germany it is now a twenty-four bedded unit, with two labour wards and an ante-natal clinic attached.

At all hours of the day and night a group of women can be seen walking along the broad, straight road leading up past the church to the hospital. It is a five-mile walk for those who live at the far end of the town. One of the women in the group is obviously in labour. She walks slowly, heavily, and stops every now and again as a strong contraction grips her. At night, a man carrying a hurricane lantern often accompanies the women, and sometimes a young man will bring his wife on the cross-bar of his bicycle. Other people will hire traders' lorries or call for the hospital truck. I look forward to the day when tribal or government money is used for the development of an ambulance service in our town.

Not all women who set off on the long walk reach the hospital. Dikeledi did not. It was July, midwinter, and the night was frosty. Dikeledi in her third pregnancy set off to walk to the hospital as soon as she was sure that she was in labour. Her mother walked with her, anxiously watching as the pains increased in intensity. About a hundred yards from the hospital she could go no farther. The labour pains gripped her and the birth was imminent. She went to the side of the road and lay down behind a small thorn bush. Her mother ran up the road as fast as she could and breathlessly called the night nurses. As the night driver was off duty, I threw on some clothes and drove with a nurse and the anxious mother down the road. We stopped at the place where Dikeledi had left the road and searched with our torches among the bushes. We heard a feeble cry, a baby's cry, and all rushed in that direction. Dikeledi was lying shivering on the frosty ground and in front of her a beautiful baby girl was yelling for all she was worth in the still frosty air. As we reached her, Dikeledi gave a push and out came the after-birth. Her mother was pleased. 'Now we can safely cut the cord,' she said. 'I don't like what I hear about you in the hospital, cutting the cord before the placenta is born.'

Many times, of course, in my visits to home confinements I had seen that the old women never cut the cord until both babe and after-birth were born. If the placenta is delayed, the babe is just left lying on the floor until at last the placenta arrives. This is no doubt a safer method than cutting the cord too quickly and it certainly ensures that all available blood from the mother passes into the baby's body. The old mid-wives, most of whom are old women who have picked up their little knowledge through years of watching women in labour, cut the cord by means of a razor blade. The cord is then left untied, the baby wrapped in a blanket and, tradi-tionally, the placenta is buried in the hut beneath the place where the mother will lie.

The nurse tied and cut the cord of Dikeledi's baby with sterile scissors. The babe was given to Dikeledi, who, shivering violently, was covered with blankets and helped on to the back of the lorry. 'I'll call this child Mmaserame, "Mother of cold",' muttered Dikeledi. Dikeledi's mother was too busy dealing with the placenta to bother about Dikeledi or the baby. She had wrapped the placenta up in her apron to take it home for burial, and she was down on her hands and knees, scraping together all the bloodstained earth, which she then buried carefully in the ground, so that not a sign of blood or of the birth remained. On my asking her why she was so particular about this, she muttered, 'Setswana doctors love to obtain pieces of placenta or human birth blood for their medicines.' When Dikeledi's mother was quite satisfied that not a sign of the birth remained, she politely but definitely requested me to take Dikeledi and the babe home. 'God has helped her,' she explained. 'She does not need your hospital now.'

There is a fallacy, widely believed by white people, that African women give birth easily, painlessly, and without complications. This is far from the truth. Certainly they are more stoical, braver, more disciplined to endure pain than their white sisters, but difficulties and complications occur just as they do with European women. Time and again suffering is alleviated and death defeated in our labour wards, and there is no greater thrill for medical and nursing staff than to see a live baby born, perhaps with instruments or by operation, after a long and trying labour.

THE LONG CONFINEMENT

On the third or fourth day, or before that if the beds are needed, our normal cases are taken home. Goitsemodimo was ready to go home long before the truck came for her and other patients at 7.30 a.m. She sat on the edge of the bed, babe at the breast, longing to reach home. When the lorry did arrive she climbed quickly on the back, and as the custom is, covered herself with her blanket so that only her eyes peeped out. Women in confinement must not be seen by strangers. Her mother was waiting for her at home. She came running forward, chuckling with delight and fussing round the truck like an old hen. She shouted, 'Thank you, thank you,' to the driver, wrapped the babe up in a blanket, pulled Goitsemodimo's blanket farther over her face and led her to the small hut at the back of the courtyard, where Goitsemodimo was to spend her two to three months of confinement.

Goitsemodimo actually spent a full two months in confinement. Many women spend three months, but the tendency today is to cut down the long period of confinement, especially among the educated people. There is much to be said for this long period. The young mother's mind is at rest, lactation seldom fails, and the baby thrives in the security of a happy child–mother relationship. But the Botswana way of life is fast changing, with many young women working as teachers, typists, and nurses. Life for many is passing from a subsistence economy to a monetary one, with the result that many young women rebel against the idea of two or three months' inactivity, and prefer the Western idea of a rapid return to work and social activities. Often in this new way of life we are asked for contraceptive advice and we use the 'pill' and the 'loop' regularly to allow the modern woman to re-enter her society more quickly and without fear of another immediate pregnancy.

The two months confinement were happy ones for Goitsemodimo. The first month is always known as the 'month of rejoicing'. Goitsemodimo lay happily in her hut with the child at her breast. It never left the warmth and comfort of the mother's side. Goitsemodimo began to gain weight; she had no worries, her milk was plentiful, and her baby grew rapidly. Babe and mother lay together in sweet contentment.

Each day Goitsemodimo's mother made maize-meal porridge for breakfast and millet porridge, *bogobe*, for other meals. The young mother was encouraged to eat as much as she could and at frequent intervals. She had her own eating utensils, used by no one else, and she did not touch her bowls with her hand. When eating her thin maize-meal porridge she would hold the bowl with a cloth over her hand. Her husband killed a goat for her, the head and innards of which he gave to Goitsemodimo's father. Rapidly she grew fat in this idyllic life of eating, sleeping, chatting with relatives, and feeding her baby. During these two months of confinement her husband lived a celibate life, for he had been warned by the old people that any unfaithfulness on his part could cause his child to become an invalid.

At last the day came for Goitsemodimo to be brought out of confinement. As usual it was a Sunday. She washed herself, rubbed face-cream into her bulging cheeks, and dressed herself in the bright new dress especially bought for her by her husband. The baby, too, was carefully washed and dressed in a new and expensive dress, while on its head was a large shady bonnet. Meanwhile, Goitsemodimo's mother and sisters had baked cakes and scones, and bought a few loaves of bread from the Indian bakery. Kettles of tea were brewed, cups and saucers borrowed from neighbours and all was ready for the coming-out tea. Relatives and friends arrived in the afternoon and were given chairs or skin mats on which to sit. Goitsemodimo was brought out of the hut with her baby for all to see. She had put on nearly two stone in weight, her complexion was pale, due to her two months' confinement in

48

the hut, but she was healthy, radiant, and happy. Everyone admired her and the baby.

'How fat she is and so beautiful; her husband has fed her well.'

'What a beautiful baby, so pretty and chubby. Look, she has her father's ears!'

After tea the deacon read the scriptures and prayed for the child and the family. Then the father announced the name. The child was to be called Malebogo, meaning 'Thanks'. All agreed that God had indeed been good and that thanks were due to him. That night Goitsemodimo, her husband, and child moved to the better hut in the front of the courtyard, and married life began again.

6

CAPTAIN OF THE MEN OF DEATH

Tuberculosis is still the greatest medical problem facing Botswana. No other disease causes so much morbidity or mortality. It is the greatest deceiver, presenting itself in many forms; affecting lungs, glands, kidneys, intestines, bones, joints, covering membranes of heart and lungs, and the central nervous system. Whenever a patient complains of cough or weakness or fever or swelling, we say, 'This is tuberculosis until proved otherwise.'

The tragedy is that this is largely a preventable disease and a curable disease. It is not prevented because of lack of funds. It would cost a great deal to vaccinate all the people of the country against tuberculosis, although the expense is negligible compared to the money spent in Britain on football pools or bird seed! Some day, with the help of the World Health Organization, such a campaign will be undertaken, but in the meantime we content ourselves with vaccinating the babies who happen to be born in hospital and some schoolchildren and nurses. The disease is not cured because of the semi-nomadic life of the people, and because there is as yet no legislation making treatment compulsory.

Before the advent of the modern drugs for treatment of this disease we used to say to the patient, 'Go away to your cattle post, where you can drink plenty of milk.' We knew that, within a few months, the diseased lungs would give up the struggle and death would come as a merciful release from the constant coughing. We knew, too, that far away at the cattle post there was less likelihood for the disease to be widely disseminated among relatives and children than in the crowded town.

Johannes was a man of about forty years of age. Frequently since the age of seventeen he had gone regularly to the gold mines of Johannesburg on a nine months' contract. Eventually, in spite of the stringent precautions which are taken by the Witwatersrand mining companies, the fine dust weakened his lungs, and tuberculosis developed. He was sent home from the mines, after his condition had been diagnosed, with a miniature X-ray and strict instructions to report to his home doctor as soon as he arrived. He was also told that since pneumoconiosis had predisposed his lung to infection he would be paid compensation by the mining company.

Johannes arrived in Molepolole early in May, a busy month for farmers, when the beans are ready for gathering and when the birds devouring the ripening corn require constant attention. His wife and family were far away at the lands, and so, finding no one at home, Johannes made his way to his lands where he found his wife and family. He stayed some weeks at the lands, enjoying the company of his wife and children, helping in the fields, and chatting with his friends over a 'calabash' of beer. Each day his cough became a little worse.

The hut at the lands was small, dark, dusty, and windowless. Johannes slept there with his wife and his youngest children, and during the night expectorated his copious sputum into an empty milk tin filled with soil and placed by his bed. The air in the tiny hut was filled with the deadly rod-shaped germs of tuberculosis. The children inhaled them when they breathed and ate them in their food, while flies carried the germs to nearby huts. The dust of the dark hut suited the germs fine and they thrived. After a couple of months Johannes visited his cattle post, some ten miles away. His eldest son, a lad of fourteen years was there. Johannes was thrilled to see and count his cattle, and he delayed there several weeks. Meanwhile his cough grew worse and sometimes as he lay in the hut at night with his son and several other boys, he could scarcely breathe and the sputum became more and more copious.

One day Johannes coughed up some blood. That really

scared him and he remembered the letter from the hospital and the tiny X-ray plate in his jacket pocket. It was now August, cold winds were blowing, and Johannes went at last to see the doctor. The miniature X-ray clearly showed disease of both lungs, and the fresh plate taken at the hospital showed that in the intervening months the disease had spread widely, so that both lungs were extensively involved.

I spoke sternly to Johannes. 'You have wasted four months of treatment. Now the disease is very severe. You must come into hospital for at least six months of treatment.'

Johannes was contrite and submissive. The coughing of blood had given him a real fright. 'All right, Doctor, I shall do just as you say. I'm very ill.'

Treatment was commenced. The wonder drugs against tuberculosis were given in concentrated dosage; one by daily injection and the others by mouth, many of them, so that Johannes lost count of the number of pills he had to swallow every day. Vitamins, tonics, and cough mixtures were also given, together with a good diet. Gradually the fever subsided, his weight increased, and the amount of sputum lessened. Still, on microscopic examination, the thin red rods of tubercle bacilli were seen in the sputum. The disease was still active and infectious.

Then one morning on the ward round I noticed that Johannes' face was dark and troubled and he was sitting straight upright in bed, as a patient will do when he has something important to say. 'What is troubling you, Johannes?' I asked.

'My wife has been to tell me that our youngest child aged three years has died,' he replied.

'Of what did the child die?' I asked.

'I do not know. My wife said that for some time he had been coughing and becoming very thin. Now I must go home for a few days. I will return without delay.'

I knew from past experience that to argue was useless. Johannes had to see to the funeral arrangements and afterwards he and his wife had to be given medicine for cleansing by the Tswana doctor. I knew that I could argue all day with Johannes about the inadvisability of going home at this point in his treatment. He would merely say, 'I understand what you say, Doctor. You speak well, but I must go home. I am needed at home.'

We gave him pills, sufficient for a week's treatment, and we impressed upon him the seriousness of failing to return for proper treatment. He assured us that nothing would prevent his being back in hospital within a week.

THE RAINS CAME

He meant what he said, but the rains came. It was not his fault that God sent the rains at that time. The day after Johannes laid his child to rest in the tribal burial ground, a steady rain commenced and continued for a week. It was the rain sent by God for people to use for ploughing. If one missed this opportunity it might be too late for ploughing and then what would a man's wife and family do in the months ahead? Johannes went out with his people to his farm to plough. He ploughed a large field and sowed millet, and then some more rain came. Johannes ploughed again and sowed beans, maize, pumpkins, and water-melons. Then he feared to leave his lands. He thought of the harvest, the beans to eat day after day, the water-melons to drink, and above all he thought of the millet which made such lovely *bogobe* and delicious bitter beer to drink. 'If I am away in hospital all these months the wife and children might become lazy and let the birds eat the crops, and in any case I feel better.'

So Johannes communed with himself and six months slipped by. Gradually the coughing became severe again and the sputum, which was drying up in hospital, came profuse once more. And if he could have seen his sputum under the microscope he would have seen those dreadful enemies of man, the rod-shaped, red-stained tubercle bacilli, steadily increasing in number. The army of the Captain of the Men of Death was slowly but surely eating away his neglected lungs.

We had long since given Johannes' bed to another needy admission. Then one day a wagon arrived with Johannes lying on a mattress in its centre. He was just skin and bone, desperately ill and coughing blood. Once again he was admitted to hospital and we fought for his life. We sent his sputum to Johannesburg for sensitivity tests and the report came back as we had feared: 'The tubercle bacillus from this case is resistant to all three drugs being used.' We kept him alive for a month and then he gradually sank into a coma and died.

THEN—HIS WIFE AND SON

Some weeks after, Johannes' wife came to the clinic with her two youngest children. The younger had a large ulcerating swelling in the left side of the neck. I felt the swollen tubercular glands, matted together beneath the skin, and I saw the discharging pus. The child was admitted to hospital with tubercular adenitis and stayed with us for nine months, during which time the ulcerating mass of glands gradually healed. The other child, a boy of ten years, was thin and weak and running a high fever. I heard the crackles of diseased lung beneath my stethoscope and I realized that the germs that had killed Johannes were now working havoc in the lungs of his child. Again we sent a specimen of the boy's sputum to Johannesburg and the report came back as we had feared and expected: 'The bacillus is resistant to all three drugs being used.' The sins of neglect of the father were being visited upon his child. Within two months the little boy lay next to his father in the tribal burial ground.

But still the deadly germ had not finished its work of destruction. We found a focus of active disease in Johannes' wife. She was, fortunately, admitted early to hospital and treatment was commenced with more expensive, 'second line' drugs. She responded to these and her life was spared.

Then one day from a distant cattle post an ox-drawn sledge arrived at the hospital. On it lay a youth, thin, pale, and paralysed from the waist downwards. We looked at his back and there over the middle of his spine was a tell-tale swelling. This was Johannes' eldest son, afflicted with tuberculosis of the spine. The diseased bone, one of the vertebrae, had collapsed, crushing the spinal cord which ran through the bone and causing paralysis below that point. We nursed him for many months, in plaster jackets, and we treated the infection with all the drugs available, and gradually the diseased bone healed and hardened, and feeling came back into the crushed nerves. He walked out of the hospital, but his legs were shaky and he was a hunchback. He would never, like his father, go to work in the gold mines.

Ignorance, neglect, and folly are the three allies of this dread disease. Its incidence is still alarmingly high, especially in the far Kalahari villages where supervision of patients is difficult. Eventually this disease will be conquered as funds for more widespread vaccination campaigns become available, and the Batswana come to realize the importance of prolonged treatment. Till that day comes, we vaccinate the new-born babies, we educate the people about the spread of the disease, and we teach the importance of submitting to prolonged months of treatment. Our sixty-bedded tuberculosis ward will be full for many years yet, but one day, in the future, it will, like the tuberculosis wards in Britain, be empty of such cases and used for the nursing of other diseases.

7

UNDER THE CANOPY OF NIGHT

On the northern boundary of Bakwena country is the village of Lephepe, one of the oldest villages in the area. I always enjoy the trip to this village, perhaps because of its historical associations with Livingstone and Moffat, who used to water their cattle at the wells there, and because of the wild country through which one drives to reach it.

I took the five-ton Bedford as I always like to do on this particular village trip, as there are usually people requiring lifts. We loaded up with drums of diesel fuel and water; bedding rolls, food boxes; medicine boxes followed; tools and spare parts for the truck, and, of course, a spade and axe, without which we never travel. Torches and lamps are essential. The driver, Station by name, busied himself around the truck. 'Have you got some patches for mending punctures?' I asked him. 'Oh yes, of course, Doctor,' he replied. 'Let me see them.' He looked for them and then remembered they were in another vehicle. We once had to patch our tube with elastoplast!

On the back of the lorry the staff nurse and cook were huddled, invisible under a pile of blankets, while the rest of the passengers sat huddled together with their blankets around them. We headed north, ninety miles of hard driving through thick sand. The road twisted and turned through farmland, climbing over jagged limestone rocks in places, bush-crashing through thorn scrub in other places. Fine dust rose in clouds, settling on us all. Here and there Station, with infinite patience, guided the huge lorry down and up steep banks of dry river-beds. The chassis creaked as it twisted from side to side; the wheels bounced furiously as the rocks threw them into the air. Every now and again, as the truck passed beneath a sprawling thorn tree, Station would give a shout of warning and the passengers on the back would flatten themselves to avoid being scratched by the long vicious thorns.

After some two hours of this type of travel we reached an area of pure sand—dirty, brown sand. Not a blade of grass or a bush could be seen. In the distance was a bore-hole, well known for its excellent supply of water. Hundreds of goats, cattle, and sheep had churned the ground up into this dust-bowl as they came day after day to water. At the watering-point we found hundreds of cattle milling around. Old men in ex-army coats thrown loosely over their shoulders, and small naked herd-boys were watering the stock, a dozen beasts at a time. The cattle were thin and ill-looking; their bones stuck through their skins frighteningly. The drought had left little for them to eat.

DIGGING OUT THE TRUCK

After some miles, the sandy plains gave place to woodland, with undulating sandy hills. Ancient gnarled trees with thick barks and huge pods hanging from the branches lifted up their crooked branches to the clear blue sky. With their thick bark and jagged thorns these camel thorn trees were able to keep alive and grow slowly over many years in the burning desert heat. Their strong roots slowly pierced their way through the sand into the limestone rock beneath which little collections of water were held by the impervious stone.

The great truck crawled slowly forwards in extra low gear. I opened the door and looked down at the track below. I saw the wheel slowly move past a piece of grass. It was travelling an inch at a time, desperately slowly, but we were still moving. Then we came to a standstill. I jumped out and saw the back wheels spinning in the sand, sinking deeper and deeper. The back axle was touching the hot sand and I could smell the burning rubber of the tyres. Station climbed slowly out of the cab and shouted to the passengers to dismount. Everyone jumped off the truck and all gazed at the wheels held fast in deep sand. Then work began.

Some dug round the wheels with the spade we carried;

others took the axe and chopped small bushes and branches to put under the wheels. Station crawled on his belly an inch at a time under the lorry, easing himself slowly into the narrow space between the rear of the lorry and the road. In one hand he dragged a heavy jack, and in the other, a flat stone which he had prudently brought with him to support the jack in the loose sand. He laid the stone flat on the sand and with much grunting and groaning he managed, with great patience and skill, to fix the jack beneath the rear wheel and the stone. The lorry was then raised until the back wheels were just a few inches out of their rut. At once branches were packed beneath the wheels and the jack released. The process was repeated several times until the axle was quite clear of the sand and the wheels were well out of the hole they had dug. In the meantime, the women had been laying branches and bushes across the tracks in front of the lorry. We all worked hard for an hour, sweating profusely and each shouting encouragement to the other! At last Station was satisfied.

'God will help us,' he said, 'let us try now.'

We all took our places round the truck, men and women alike, for every ounce of forward propulsion would help to move it. Slowly and carefully, as a mother would coax a fractious child, Station eased the truck forwards and then, when he knew the back wheels were out of their self-dug holes, he gave it full throttle. Whenever he felt the wheels spinning he slowed the engine down, not like an inexperienced driver who would rev up the engine, burn out the clutch and spin the wheels deep into the sand! We all pushed hard, those at the rear of the truck were covered in flying sand that shot up from the spinning wheels.

We shouted and pushed, and then, very slowly, the lorry moved forward, gathering momentum, and carried itself over the sandy rise. Only when the truck was safely over the rise did Station dare to stop it and wait for us to catch up to him, puffing and blowing for all we were worth. A large secretary-bird, with its quill-like head feathers, strode away from us with an ungainly appearance as if offended that we had disturbed its desert home. We passed another bore-hole from which a line of women carrying pails of water on their heads moved. As they walked they shouted to each other, not daring to turn round to speak directly to each other in case the water spilt.

DESERT CLINICS

The village of Boatlaname consists of a couple of dozen huts stretched out on a rocky, barren hillside. We stopped at the Headman's hut, and after the usual words of greeting, he and I stood together looking out on a vast, wide valley before us stretching to the far north. A year or two ago I had stood with him on this very spot, gazing upon acre after acre of ripening millet, and I remembered saying to him, 'What a fine harvest you have this year!' Perhaps his reply was typical of farmers the world over, as he gazed slowly over his fields with eyes screwed tight in the bright sunshine. 'Yes,' he said, 'I suppose you are right. It could be better, but we will at least have a little food to put in our mouths.' As he said this he made a gesture of eating porridge with his hand. Today, however, the fields were bare and barren, a veritable dust-bowl. He turned sorrowfully towards his huts saying, 'I've prepared a hut for use as a clinic.'

He showed me a small hut at the back of his courtyard, where a small group of women and children were sitting patiently waiting, each with a bottle clutched in the hand. These were Bakwena people from Molepolole who spent most of their time among their stock and farms at Boatlaname. Some of them were quite high-born Bakwena. The small hut, although dark, was clean and freshly smeared. A pail of water stood ready, together with a small, rickety home-made table and two low Setswana stools. The nurse called the patients in one at a time for examination. Each then laid their prescription paper on the floor with bottle on top of it for the nurse to fill. I gave vitamin syrup to the under-nourished children, vitamin pills and tonics to the pregnant women, sulphur ointment for the cases of scabies, and cough mixtures for the chronic coughs. Laxative pills were handed out liberally and gratefully received. Penicillin was given by injection to the venereal disease cases and to the children with acute infections.

Everyone wanted as much medicine and pills as they could persuade me to give. They knew a month would pass before another visit by the doctor was to be made. Outside in the courtyard, hens cackled, children played happily, and grateful patients chatted quietly to one another. One old man took a long swig at his bottle of medicine and then passed it round his wife and children for each to have a good drink. Near by, some girls were stamping corn for the evening meal and a few old men were sitting idly in the *kgotla*. After the last patient had been seen, we packed our medicine boxes, enjoyed a cup of tea which Win, my wife, and Sesupo, the cook, had organized, and then reloaded the truck and headed north again. We passed through wooded country, with fertile soil, passing herds of cattle and barren farmlands until we reached the next village of Sojwe.

This was a larger village than the last, a village of Makgalagadi people, uneducated and very noisy. A large crowd of patients had gathered at the Headman's hut. The routine was repeated, boxes off-loaded and carried into the small hut, water for diluting the stock mixtures placed by the boxes in the hut. A brief Bible reading and prayer, and then one by one the excited patients came into the hut. All who did not receive an injection went away dissatisfied. Each received a bottle of medicine, and many went away with pills, ointment, eye-drops, and so forth, as well. It was backbreaking work for the nurse, who filled the bottles placed on the floor from the stock mixtures. Between filling bottles and dispensing pills she gave injections, trying her best to keep the fine dust from the unsmeared floor from contaminating her sterile syringes.

The village of Lephepe stands in a sea of deep sand, sand that is brown in colour and mixed with the dried excreta of hundreds of sheep, goats, and cattle. After a shower of rain numerous weeds, all with burrs or sharp thorns, appear spreading over the ground and making walking difficult and unpleasant. Woollen socks are covered with irritating seeds and sticky burrs. A couple of hundred or so closely built huts comprise the town, together with an old mud-walled church, a newly erected school, and a trader's store.

We drove to the church and off-loaded the lorry. At one end of the small church was a low mud platform with a pulpit cleverly made out of dried mud, topped with a reading board made out of an old packing case. Pieces of wood from packing cases were used to close the windows which were without glass. Neither of the two doors into the church would close properly, so that goats and hens could wander in and out as they chose. The local women had smeared the floor with fresh mud and cow dung in anticipation of our visit, and several pails of water had been placed ready for our use. Rough, friendly hands grasped ours, and happy faces smiled a welcome. The Headman, an old Molepolole man, was there, the pastor, the schoolteacher, the tax collector, a cattle inspector, and an agricultural demonstrator. All were homesick for Molepolole and asked about their friends and relatives. A group of local church women, friendly and excited, chatted to my wife and the nurse.

Before the sun went down and darkness descended like a blanket, we had seen a couple of dozen patients and arranged to take several back to hospital with us on the morrow. With the darkness came the cold.

STARS AND SATELLITES

The fire drew us all to its warmth and we brought our chairs as near as we could. The sky was clear and a million stars looked down upon us. The Southern Cross showed us the direction from which we had come, while low down in the northern sky we could just see the Plough. The dark hole in the Milky Way could be seen clearly; the Seven Sisters looked cold as they huddled together, and, as always, Venus, the evening star, smiled down upon us, 'asking for supper'. Two satellites, only slightly more brilliant than the stars, moved slowly and smoothly across the sky; one from east to west and one from north to south: one American and one Russian. How far away we seemed from the intrigues of east and west, as we sat there by the fire talking with people who

never read a newspaper and who were just beginning to realize a little of the great world outside! How strange that here,
in the heart of Africa, amid the silences of the vast Kalahari,
the cold war, the power struggle, the fears and jealousies of
the great powers, were all brought vividly before us by those
two silent travellers across the heavens!

I always love this time round the evening fire. The soft
noises of the village are in the background, the faint hum of
voices, the occasional cry of a child, the bark of a dog, the
distant singing of a group of dancing youths, the stamp of
oxen's feet in the kraal, the cackle of hens as they settle down
for the night in the branches of a thorn tree. The day's work
is done, the hospital with its telephone is far away, no letters to
answer, one gazes dreamily into the fire, relaxed, warm,
comfortable. Every now and again someone adjusts the dry
wood, pushing a log further into the fire or throwing on
some brushwood to give added light and heat; fresh logs are
placed like the spokes of a wheel round the fire ready to be
pushed in as the flames demand.

The village pastor, sincere, devout, although with little
education, told me of his problems in the church; of petty
jealousies, of rival claims to leadership; of the problems of
influencing the young people, of the hardness of the men, of
the village schoolteacher, who had recently joined a prophet
sect and now prevented the children from attending Sunday
School. He spoke of his joys, of the Headman who just recently had confessed Christ as Saviour, of the progress of his
children at school, of the goodness and devotion of his wife,
of the faithfulness of many of his flock.

Soon the talk came round to the drought. The old elder
shook his head and said, 'We pray every day for rain, but
God does not answer. I wish I knew why.'

An old woman crouching low over the fire gave the
answer. 'Look,' she said, 'you are a father with children. If
your children are playing quietly and nicely you do not take
a stick and beat them, but if they fight and quarrel, or if the
goats are lost you thrash them. So it is with God. He is beating us with his big stick of hunger because we do not live as
he wants us to live, or do as he desires. Our children do not

fear us as in the olden days when the rains came regularly. Our unmarried daughters have children; our sons are drunk. And the land is full of false prophets who make money out of the Bible; who baptize for money, who offer prayers for money, who demand money even to be seen. The chiefs also, what do they do? They quarrel and cheat. Do you wonder that God is angry and that he is beating us hard?'

Soon the pastor talked about his family and the difficulty of clothing and educating them. I had already examined his wife, now in the last month of her tenth pregnancy. I said, 'Moruti, you have many children. You will never be able to clothe and educate them all, and your wife is becoming old and worn out. Let me stop her now after this child from having more children.'

'How could I go against the will of God?' he replied. 'He will surely think me very ungracious. I fear to offend him. Nevertheless, you can talk with my wife. If you and she agree together, you can sterilize her. But as for me, I fear the God who heard my prayer and gave me children.'

Venus sank in the western sky and the Southern Cross moved slowly across the sky. The satellites appeared again, travelling round the earth with effortless ease. I thought bitterly that if I had a fraction of the money spent on those playthings of the great powers I could give the Bakwena all they needed in the way of a medical service. I gazed sadly into the fire. Suddenly the pastor rose to his feet. 'Let us pray,' he said. We bowed our heads as he spoke to God, as a child speaking to a loving father, as though God was just by his side. He poured out his heart in thanksgiving and asked for God's protection through the night. I looked at his face, and through the lines of the years of hardship, I saw, illuminated by the flickering shadows of the fire, a radiant peace: the peace of a man who lives with God.

The morning was chilly and we were glad that Station's big log had smouldered all through the night leaving a good pile of hot ash on which new dry twigs were soon blazing. We ate our breakfast of maize porridge, bread and marmalade round the fire, and we had only just finished when the pastor arrived, refreshed and ready for the day's work, complete with Bible and hymn book in his hand.

CLINIC IN THE CHURCH

'Let us have the service first, before the clinic,' he said. 'If you have the clinic first, the patients will go away without hearing the Word of God.' And so after breakfast we cleared up the church and prepared for worship. The pastor went over to a large thorn tree from which was hanging the church 'bell', the iron axle of an old cart-wheel. He removed a piece of iron from the fork of the tree and beat hard on the axle. A loud bell-like sound travelled over the village, and gradually people began to appear from all directions.

The Christian women came in their white head scarves, blouses, and black skirts, the men in their khaki trousers and jackets. Some had travelled many miles for this monthly service with the doctor. I gave a simple talk on the love of God, and the tiny congregation seemed to drink in every word I spoke. After the sermon the Sacrament of the Lord's Supper was dispensed. Then the church was transformed into a clinic.

The nurse laid out her bottles of medicine on the pews, together with her dressings, instruments, and injections. My wife helped to dispense medicines and count out pills. I sat at the rickety communion table to examine the sick, and laid those for examination on a blanket on the floor. A few I promised to take back with me to hospital; a pregnant woman with an abnormal lie; a man with tuberculosis; a child with large infected wounds; a young woman with an abdominal tumour; and a young man with advanced trachoma whose eye-lashes were rubbing on his eyes.

We finished the clinic at 2.30 p.m., hot and dirty, weary and sticky. The pastor was there waiting for us, smiling as usual. 'The church ladies have made tea for you.' A group of clean, gentle, humble-looking church women fussed about. Before each one of us they placed a large dish of curried chicken and maize corn. Then the oldest woman said, 'Let us give thanks.' She kneeled down with her head touching the ground, rather like a Mohammedan at prayer. She prayed in a fast low voice, and for so long that the food was almost cold.

Outside, the sun scorched down on a parched earth of withered crops. Food was scarce. I felt unworthy to eat it, for this was a sacrificial gift, given by hungry people out of generous and loving hearts.

We drove through the evening and the darkness of the early night. Just before midnight we reached Molepolole. The streets were deserted, the huts dark.

'Everyone is asleep,' said Station, 'can I have a day off tomorrow?'

'Yes,' I said, 'but first we must take the patients for admission and unload the truck.'

Another village trip had been accomplished and I knew that in that village ninety miles away lives had been saved, pain eased, infections killed, and a little church of believers strengthened in their faith. But I knew also that for a month there would be no medical aid for that village and I longed for the day when I could station a trained nurse there.

8

DWELLERS IN THE FAR KALAHARI

There is a point on the road west of Molepolole on the way to the large Kalahari village of Letlhakeng, where I usually say to my visitors, 'The Kalahari begins here.' It is a place where the road leaves the firm soil which has been its surface for twenty miles, and climbs a gradual rise of deep sand. Then the country opens out into wide grassy plains with thorn scrub, camel thorn trees and acacia bush. The grass is coarse, growing in long tufts out of the deep sand.

The Kalahari is called desert because for hundreds of square miles there is no surface water, only a vast expanse of flat bushland. It is, nevertheless, a beautiful bushland which captures the heart and the imagination of all who enter its interior. There is a strange magic about it which grips the heart. You feel that life has stopped for a thousand years! That the world is old and primeval and that time has no meaning.

Only the red sun by day marks the passage of the hours, and the brilliant moon by night tells of the passing months. The trees are gnarled and old, and great dead tree-trunks raise their naked branches to the sky, as they stand, hard as steel, immovable, where drought, or a flash of tropical lightning, has struck them dead. Herds of antelope, of springbok, impala, hartebeest, gnus, and the lordly eland, wander over the plains and through the leafy glades as they have done since time immemorial.

The lion roars as he follows the zebra and the herds of ugly, hump-backed gnu. The leopard crouches in his tree, waiting to spring out with untold fury upon the passing game. Packs of wild dogs chase a terrified buck, leaping cruelly at its bleeding side. Hyenas, jackals, and vultures eat what the lion leaves. And there are villages scattered in this vast bushland. Villages of Makgalagadi people, and beyond the villages are the wandering Bushmen, the Masarwa, that despised but lovable last creature of God.

Seventy miles west of Molepolole I drove the truck down a rough track over an outcrop of limestone rock on to a huge, circular salt-pan. Its surface was glaring and white in the brilliant sunshine, and in the distance we could see springbok and hartebeest licking the salt on the dry, caked surface of the pan. Such salt-pans, often three to five miles in diameter, are found scattered all over the vast Kalahari desert. They are a favourite place for game to congregate, and often a small village is found at one point on the circumference. After rains, the pans hold water for a few weeks, and at the edge of them wells are often dug by the Makgalagadi villagers. Once on the flat surface of the pan I could drive at fifty miles per hour, and as we travelled across the pan I could see lorry tracks going off in all directions, where hunters had been chasing game.

KALAHARI HEADMAN

When we reached the small church-cum-school which was to serve as clinic and sleeping quarters for our two days in the village, I noticed that old Rramaeba was waiting for me with his usual mischievous grin on his face. He was a typical Mokgalagadi headman who had come ten miles from his village deep in the dry bushland. His old wagon was standing near by and the oxen which had pulled it through the Kalahari sand were grazing not far away. He had brought his two wives, numerous children and grandchildren, and several other families on the wagon.

'Good day, Marriwedder, my, you do look well fed! You are obviously not short of food! I've come for an injection! A man's injection that will rejuvenate me! But, remember, I've no money.'

I grinned back at him and greeted him and his wives. He wore an ancient soft hat on his greying head, and a long scraggy beard like a goat's fell from his chin. His face was deeply wrinkled with age and with the years of living under a burning sun. When he spoke his front teeth, from which the gums had gradually receded, moved like long, yellow fangs. His nails were long and dirty and his nostrils snuff-filled.

Over his old torn shirt he wore a jacket which I coveted. It and his trousers were made of stenbuck skin, skilfully softened and carefully sewn to fit him. His feet were shod with sandals of eland skin, and round his neck hung a necklace of brightly coloured large beads from the bottom of which, housed in a small leather case, hung his long needle, used for sewing skins and karosses.

Rramaeba's senior wife sat next to him on the sand. She wore traditional Sekgalagadi dress, a skin skirt decorated with beads and a cloak of skin flung loosely over one shoulder. This covered one side of her chest and she could pull it round either to cover the front or the back of her chest, wherever she felt the need. Some tight wire bangles were fastened round her wrists and legs. Round her neck hung a necklace of large bright beads, from the bottom of which hung a little container, carved out of an ox horn, in which she kept her snuff. Next to this container hung a little home-made metal spoon, shaped like a tiny spade. As I stood chatting with her and her husband, she took the little metal spade, cleaned out her nose with it and then with a deft flick she sent the extracted mixture of nasal secretion and snuff flying away into the sand. She cleared out the other nostril and then, filling her palm from the snuff bottle, she inhaled deeply.

Rramaeba's junior wife was sitting a little distance away, feeding her two-year-old son at her breast, which she had, with considerable difficulty dragged out from the front of her bright yellow dress. She, like most of the Makgalagadi women, had discarded traditional skin dress to wear often ill-fitting but brightly coloured dresses. This change from skins to print material has been rapid in recent years and skin dresses will very soon be a thing of the past.

As usual, we commenced our clinic with prayers conducted by the local pastor, a Molepolole man, whose attitude to the local Makgalagadi was very sympathetic. We laid out our medicines and equipment on a bench and I sat at a home-made rickety table to see the patients. Old Rramaeba came in first.

'My kidneys and my blood are full of disease. I'm old and getting impotent. I want an injection,' he said, with a grin on his wrinkled face.

'Put your money on the table: four shillings,' I replied.

'I've no money. How can I pay when I have all these women and children to pay for?'

'Nurse,' I called. 'Put old Rramaeba outside until he sees if there is anyone from whom he can borrow some money.' The nurse advanced with a grin.

'Oh, all right,' said Rramaeba as he fished a skin wallet out of his inside pocket. It was full of notes. He extracted a five-pound note and gave it to me. I knew that there were two wives and numerous children to be paid for out of that money and so I kept the note, promising to give him the change later. Most of the other patients brought their money in their hands; others brought hens or jackal skins. All paid what they could and all hoped that their treatment would include an injection and some ointment.

IN GAME COUNTRY

That evening we drove deeper west, climbing over heavy sand dunes into wide open grassland. We were now in excellent game country and our eyes were flashing from right to left as we sorted out the various species of game. Springbok were the most common, leaping with all four legs apart, right across the road; a herd of blue wildebeest (gnus) rushed madly across the road with humped backs heaving and great clouds of dust rising behind them; here and there we saw a noble gemsbok, tall, straight, backpointing antlers giving it a kingly look; groups of khudu with their huge curved horns were glimpsed now and again, while duikers, hares, and jackals occasionally leapt across the track.

At one point we saw a crowd of vultures hovering in the air and settling on some trees. We thought that perhaps a lion had made a kill, and we drove across the bush to see what was happening. We found an ox, dead of thirst, being torn to pieces by the vultures, those great scavengers of the bush. The sun was now low in the west, soon the prowlers of the night would appear, the lion, the leopard, and the hyena.

We made our camp in a thicket of thorn bush on the edge

of the pan. From it we could gaze out across its great flat surface as smooth as a tarred road. We made up our camp-beds, and as the cold night air came down we drew our chairs round the fire and relaxed in its pleasant warmth. We all slept round the fire; some of the party on camp-beds, some on skin mats. Every now and again through the night we could hear one of the men rising to heap wood on the fire. There is nothing like a good fire to keep lions away! In the early morning, driver Station showed me the track-marks of a lion that had circled the camp. 'That is why,' he said in a most self-righteous voice, 'when you were asleep I was awake keeping the fire going.'

THE BUSHMEN APPEAR

The first Bushman appeared while we were having break-fast. He approached the fire quietly, softly, like some timid animal. He was followed by a second, older man. They squatted on their haunches by the fire, their tiny feet in the warm ash. They were both less than five feet tall, very thin, with unwashed bodies on which dust was deeply ingrained. They each wore a tiny leather girdle and, over their shoulders, each had a small skin cloak loosely flung. The Masarwa gave us friendly, open smiles from their unwashed, wrinkled faces. Many tiny scars, probably the result of witch-doctors' ad-ministrations, were over their faces and bodies, and I noticed that both of them had the watery eyes of trachoma infection. The younger of the two took out a hollow piece of bone and some tobacco leaf from a little skin bag attached to his girdle. He lit this simple pipe with a smouldering ember from the fire, inhaled deeply, and then passed on the pipe to the other man. He in turn inhaled deeply and then returned the pipe to the first man.

'I heard them singing late last night,' said Station. 'There must be a settlement of them close by our camp.'

The Masarwa settlement nearby consisted of about four bivouacs of grass and branches, very small and low, and ob-viously of a very temporary nature. Round a small fire a group of women and children were crouching. Their dress was as scanty as that of the men. The women were about four feet six inches high and their yellow bodies were deeply ingrained with dirt. They welcomed us with warm smiles, showing tiny yellow teeth, some of which had been sharpened with files. Near by, a couple of men were pegging out the skin of a hare they had just caught; its flesh was hanging in a nearby tree, covered with flies.

DIGGING FOR A DRINK

One of the Masarwa pointed to a few dried leaves on a long thin stem. He began to dig, following the thin stem into the ground. Two feet below the surface he produced a large round bulb, the size of a water-melon. He took it over to where the women were sitting round the fire and cut it into slices over a wooden basin. Fluid came out of it, which he drank. I tasted this fluid; it was bitter and astringent but it could keep a person alive when there was no surface water. He then showed me another bulb which he dug up from three feet underground. This was a large thick-skinned bulb as big as a large pumpkin. He told me that the antelopes, especially the gemsbok, dig them up and eat them for the fluid they contain. That explained how these game animals can live for months in the desert when there is no surface water. He told me that he could not drink the juice from that particular bulb, as it was greasy and very astringent. But he squeezed some into his hand and used it as a soap for washing himself.

'I'll show you how we find fluid when there is absolutely no water,' said our Masarwa friend. He scooped a small hole in the sand and then laid twigs and grass across the top. He cut open the stomach from a springbok which had just been brought in and which was being skinned. He removed the stomach contents and held them in his hands, a large ball of green stuff, half-digested grass mixed with stomach juices. He held this over his hole and squeezed hard and filtered the green fluid through the twigs and grass. Then he removed the twigs and grass, stooped down and drank with his mouth from the tiny pool of green liquid. When he stood up there was a vivid green circle round his mouth. I should imagine that one would need to be very thirsty indeed before partaking of such a drink, even though the fluid would be rich in vitamins and digestive juices!

The Masarwa, who was called Thobane by the Makgalagadi, although I doubt if that was his real Sesarwa name, then discussed hunting. He took us to the edge of the pan, where he showed me a trap he had placed there in the track of small antelopes. The noose was made of sinew, fastened to a springy branch bent over. It was cleverly camouflaged and he proudly told us that his success rate was high. Nearly every morning he found a hare or a small duiker hanging by its neck in the trap. Thobane's brother now joined us and I was most interested in the bow and arrows he carried. The bow was small, only about nine inches long, made from a supple twig with a string of sinew. The arrows were small reeds with tips of beaten metal.

The poison for the arrows is obtained from the cocoon of a certain caterpillar and its effects are like that of the drug curare; it causes muscular paralysis. Thobane told me how, with infinite patience, the hunter would crawl slowly up to an animal until he was just a few yards away, and then he would let an arrow fly. The poisonous metal tip would pierce the animal's skin and the reed shaft would fall off. In a flash the animal would be off at a furious gallop and would travel some miles before the poison took effect. The hunter would trot along after the animal following its footprints, which he could distinguish from those of other animals which had passed that way. After some hours of travelling he would come upon his prey lying paralysed or dead beneath some bush. With his spear or knife he would kill it. If the animal was a large one, such as an eland or a giraffe, the Mosarwa hunter would call his family and friends to the spot; they would make camp there, eating and engorging themselves until the animal was finished.

I think the cruellest way of hunting was the way Thobane caught hares. This method is commonly used in Botswana, not only by the Masarwa but by other people as well. Long, thin supple branches are joined together making a bendable stick about twelve feet long. To the end of this is attached a steel hook, bent back on itself like a fisherman's hook. The hunter goes to the warren of spring hares or rabbits, seals up most of the holes, and then pushes this long supple branch down the hole until its hook catches the hare, hiding at the far end of its burrow. It is then pulled out like a fish on a hook and killed at once by dogs.

I asked the Masarwa to show us how to make fire by rubbing two sticks together. I had heard that the Masarwa could do this. He produced two sticks which he obviously kept for that purpose. Both seemed to be of a very hard wood. He laid one down on the ground and then using the palms of his hands he rotated the other stick rapidly with its point on the centre of the stick which was laid on the ground. Faster and faster he rotated the vertical stick, his palms moving up and down rhythmically. Presently a wisp of smoke could be seen where the two sticks rubbed against each other. Thobane took a tiny piece of dry grass and placed it on the spot, blowing gently at the same time. The grass took light and dried leaves and more grass was added until there was a definite blaze, to which thin sticks were added, and a fire appeared before our eyes.

DEEPER INTO THE DESERT

We pushed on another seventy miles west to the village of Motokwe, through wooded areas of great gnarled trees, heat and drought resistant, over plains of long coarse grass, through thorn scrub and over flat salt pans. All day, our eyes were watching for game; once, resting among a crop of bush-covered limestone rocks we saw a lion. We reached the pan on which Motokwe lies in the late afternoon. A bore-hole had been sunk in the centre of this pan and at 300 feet a plentiful supply of fresh clear water was found. Hundreds of lowing oxen and bleating goats were milling around the bore-hole, being watered by numerous herd-boys who were bringing their herds home for the night. We took the opportunity of filling our drums with the clear water.

We camped in the little broken-down church-cum-school

building in the centre of the village of Motokwe. Pictures of President Khama and Queen Elizabeth were stuck with drawing-pins on the mud walls of the building, together with the school time-table and the pastor's preaching plan. The building was on a small rise, surrounded by a sea of deep sand in which numerous small huts with their courtyards could be seen. A thorn fence was round the building with an opening back and front, and in one corner of the enclosed yard we made our kitchen. The pastor, a Molepolole man, was there to welcome us, together with some of his church members. They had brought buckets of water, a hen, and some eggs for us.

We found a small group of patients waiting, local Makgalagadi villagers with a few Masarwa standing shyly in the background. After a cup of tea I began to examine these patients. The Masarwa held back until I had examined the Makgalagadi folk. Then they shyly approached, a couple of men, half a dozen women, and some children. The children's heads were all infected with the fungus of *witkop* and were white and thickly crusted with the disease. Several of the children were covered with the highly infectious lesions of endemic syphilis. All begged for injections.

The last to appear was Nche, who came limping in at the end. She was an attractive young woman whose pale brown skin was smooth and delicate. Her eyes were big and frightened like those of a young antelope. I saw her right ankle was swollen and from a dozen places pus was oozing out from the diseased joint. I realized that she had a severe tubercular infection of the ankle joint, and I indicated to her and her parents that I would take her to hospital. She shook her head and limped out of the tiny church. The last I saw of her was her tiny figure limping away through deep sand into the western bushland, limping away to die in the only place she knew, the cruel, scorching Kalahari.

Early next morning a large crowd of patients had gathered expectantly at the church. Many had come with relatives and friends, and there was a real holiday atmosphere about the village. The doctor had arrived for his quarterly visit and he was sure to have drinking medicines, injections, ointments, and pills. This was a day not to be missed, a day to have an injection, to lay in a supply of pills, a day to be examined, whether you were really ill or not, for when the doctor departed and returned whence he had come, 200 miles to the east, no one could be sure when he would return. The people sat about in small groups, chattering excitedly among themselves. Most of them were Makgalagadi, the women wearing bright, ill-fitting loose dresses, and the men, dull khaki skirts with buckskin trousers.

Under a tree near the school the teacher had taken his classes for the day, kindly vacating the small building for use as a clinic. He was a young, educated man from Molepolole, and he, his wife and family had recently settled in this far-off village. He had a real sense of vocation, and under difficult conditions was trying to educate the Makgalagadi children. There were about forty of them, bright-eyed youngsters, in his school, the girls dressed in gym tunics and the boys in khaki shorts and shirts. They sang for us in loud, raucous voices, first a hymn, then a Setswana song, and finally the Botswana National Anthem. I congratulated the teacher on his efforts, and the pastor, also a Molepolole man, put in a word, saying that not only did the teacher help the children during the week, but never missed having a Sunday School with them.

'GONE TO NOAH'S CHURCH'

The day began with a service. Everyone packed themselves into the tiny church, the Chief's representative, the teacher and his wife, the staff nurse, and my wife being given seats of honour alongside the pulpit, while the deacons sat in the front row. The rest of the congregation sat on the mud floor, and last of all the pastor pushed in a group of skin-clad Masarwa who sat in an embarrassed circle on the floor, looking at each other with expressionless faces. Hymns were sung, out of tune, and with loud high-pitched voices. The pastor preached long and earnestly, urging the people to repent and believe. In the middle of his sermon a woman fell stiffly to the floor, uttering, loud, piercing hysterical screams. A

75

couple of deacons took her gently outside the church where her cries gradually subsided. 'The Spirit has come upon her,' the pastor explained to me. 'She has been a bad woman, now she will be a Christian.' Later the pastor talked to her and invited her to join his training class for church membership.

The preaching ended, the mass of the people left the church, leaving only the full members of the church, a few women in white blouses, a few old men, the teacher, and the Chief's representative. I administered the Sacrament of Holy Communion to these simple believers deep in the Kalahari desert. Before they drank the wine they had to shake the flies off the cup, while I noticed my wife extracting two, swimming furiously, in her tiny cup. I watched the gnarled fingers take the bread and lift the cup. I saw a look of peace and rapture on the wrinkled faces of those old Makgalagadi believers, as Christ's shed Blood and broken Body fed their hungry souls. Christ's Sacrifice had united us all together, there in that lonely, barren spot, a little group of whites, of pure Bakwena, and of humble Makgalagadi. We felt as one in him and I knew again that he and he alone can bring white and black together in this great continent.

After the Sacrament, before the congregation dispersed, the pastor asked me to go through the Church roll. He handed me a tattered exercise book from which I called out the names of his members.

'Where is Montsho?' 'Oh, he is dead. He coughed blood until he died.'

'Where is Ranko?' 'Oh, he has gone to Noah's church.'

'Where is Mosadithebe?' 'She had a baby while her husband was at the mines and has been suspended from membership.'

'Where is Mmamosweu?' 'Oh, she has gone to Noah.'

'Where is Maria?' 'She too has gone to Noah's church.'

'Where is Basadibotlhe?' 'She has gone to Noah and says she won't come back to us.'

They told me of Noah's church. It was an indigenous church, founded by the hereditary Makgalagadi headman of this village, who wanted his people to be free from the dominion of the Bakwena. He called the people to flee to his church, a place of refuge for all Makgalagadi, as Noah's ark was a place of refuge at the time of the flood. He was a prophet and priest, called by God, to save his Makgalagadi friends from the tyranny of their Bakwena lords, and the fire of an ardent nationalism burned in his breast as he sailed his ark over the Kalahari sands. We heard his congregation singing and dancing late that night, the deep bass of the men's voices carried through the night air as they harmonized with the shrill voices of the women.

We heard the clap of hands and the thud of stamping feet, and between the songs of praise we heard long and passionate prayers in which the prophet called upon God to bless the Makgalagadi people. Then he preached, shouting in ecstasy, telling the simple people of the deliverance he was bringing to them. He told them of his power to heal, he baptized them with water, dirty, salty but holy, and he gave them holy water to drink or to tie around their necks in small bottles. They seemed to be finding an outlet for their emotions and feelings which was denied them in the orthodox missionary church, and for them religion was a live, throbbing, ardent affair to be enjoyed by all. And when the prophet killed an ox which they all ate together, religion became for them a joyous, happy affair!

TWO HUNDRED PATIENTS

As soon as the service was over the staff nurse laid out her clinic, wrote cards for the two hundred or so patients who had by this time arrived, and we set to work. The Chief's representative, the teacher, the pastor, and their wives and children appeared first in that order of seniority. When they had all been dealt with, we began to examine the Makgalagadi. They were terribly excited and the noise of their shouting made it difficult to hear anything through my stethoscope. The nurse and I worked hard, seeing the great crowd of patients as quickly as was reasonably possible. We pulled teeth, we incised abscesses, we stitched assault wounds, we palpated pregnant women, we listened to tubercular chests, we felt swellings in various places, we gave penicillin injections,

77

and my wife helped us to hand out pills, medicines, and ointments.

When all the Makgalagadi patients had been seen, we began
to pack up for the return journey. Then I saw him: a little
Mosarwa boy being dragged through the deep sand by a
wealthy Makgalagadi man. When he reached the church
I could see the child's heart flapping wildly between his ribs.
His breath came in short sharp gasps, almost too rapid to
count. It was the deep sand on the gentle slope up to the
church that had tested his puny strength to the limit. The
last hundred yards had been too much for the tiny lungs,
eaten away with advanced tuberculosis, and for a heart
weakened by toxaemia and anaemia.

Rrapula pulled the small child to the nurse and gave her
four shillings. 'Write this child's name in your book, it is my
servant's child, but his father has died and his mother has run
away with the Masarwa. Call him "Modise".' He was a thin
child of some six years of age, standing with an expressionless
face, gasping for breath. His body was unwashed and round
his waist was a tiny piece of animal skin, his only wordly
possession. I put the stethoscope gently on the heaving chest
and heard dreadful crackles over both lungs and deeply echo-
ing breath sounds, like wind blowing over the mouths of
great caves, telling of lungs eaten away into great abscesses
full of tubercular pus. Through all the noise of his breathing
I could hear in the background the rapid galloping sounds of
his failing heart. Of course, I knew he would die. He would
die unloved and uncared for and then be buried like an animal under a bush in the Kalahari.

KALAHARI WAIF

Then within myself I said, 'I'll fight for him and save his
life. I'll give him all the mighty drugs of modern medicine,
digitalis, cortisone, streptomycin, vitamins, proteins, nursing
care, and love that he needs so much. He who has known
nothing but a goat-skin for a bed will sleep in a cot of spotless
sheets, soft and clean. He who has known hunger all his
days, eating once a day or twice if lucky, will have three

good meals a day. He who knows no mother's love, no father's care, will be surrounded by the loving care of devoted nurses. This child will live and know the joy of life.' 'Nurse, we'll take this child to hospital.' The lorry was already loaded for the long journey home. Baikgatlhi, the warm-hearted nurse, climbed on to the back of the five-tonner and eased her massive figure down among the bedding rolls and boxes. 'Give me the child,' she said. The Bushman child was lifted gently into her ample bosom. 'Look!' said some Makgalagadi women standing behind me, 'he's taking a dog back with him.'

For two days and two nights the Bushman boy was cared for by the nurse. He coughed continuously, he sweated profusely, he was delirious at night, he ate food greedily with his thin, dirt-ingrained hands. His eyes followed the nurse in all her movements. She, in turn cared for him as her own child. Half the night he sat by the camp-fire struggling for breath. Never a word did he speak.

At the hospital, willing hands lifted him into a clean bed. He lay on a soft mattress, he was fed three times a day and frequently powerful medicines were given. All the skill of modern medical science was his. 'The cortisone will give the tuberculosis drugs time to work,' I thought to myself. Then one day he smiled; then he spoke and he began to learn Setswana. He began to enjoy life and he responded to love and security.

'I've done it,' I prided myself on the ward round one day. 'He'll live.' But the stethoscope revealed the crackling crepitations of active disease and the cavernous sounds of a destroyed lung.

On Sundays his cot was brought with the other children to the little hospital Sunday School. He sang choruses and learned to pray. He could say the name, 'Jesus'.

The end came suddenly one evening. The nurse called me and gave oxygen and stimulants, but when I reached his cot he had gone. But there was a faint smile on the drawn, yellow face, and I knew that the 'dog of the Kalahari' had seen the love of God in the mission hospital and that the little soul had fled to everlasting joy.

I asked the tribal authorities where he could be buried and tactfully they explained that as this was a Mosarwa, and 'not a person' he could not be buried in the tribal burial ground. They suggested outside the hospital fence. We dug a tiny grave outside the west gate of the hospital, into which we gently lowered the little body, wrapped in a white sheet. We prayed over the lonely grave, a sister from Scotland, Baikgatlhi his nurse, a labourer, and I. Then we shovelled in the earth and piled a heap of stones over the grave. Two days later it was reported that the grave had been opened and we found that part of the body had been taken away, for medicine, perhaps. We closed in the grave again and placed large, heavy stones on the top.

Note on the Masarwa

The Masarwa are, of course, objects of great interest, living as they do as man did in the dawn of time. So, year by year, expeditions come from the universities of America, Britain, and South Africa. They come with their land-rovers, chevrolet trucks, scientific equipment, with cameras and rifles. They come to study the teeth, the skin, the bones, the genitalia, the temperature, the blood groups of the Masarwa. They give them tobacco, money, food, and sweets, and they take photographs and hunt game and have a wonderful holiday in the vast unknown bushland called the Kalahari. Then they return to their universities and write a paper and plan another trip.

In view of all this scientific interest in the Masarwa, the British government before Independence appointed a young British officer as District Commissioner for the Central Kalahari, with special instructions to make a detailed study of the Masarwa and their way of life. This young officer lived closely with the Bushmen for a couple of years and produced a most instructive and helpful document in which he recommended that a central Kalahari Bushman reserve be established, with bore-holes to supply water for this lovely people. In 1967 the government of Botswana passed an act which gives protection to the Masarwa from exploitation. In terms of this bill, expeditions and people wishing to study and photograph the Masarwa must obtain the permission of the Minister of Home Affairs before they go into Bushmen areas. In the far west near the South West African border, the Dutch Reformed Church has started a mission and a school among the Masarwa. There, and in the

Bamangwato area to the north, many of them are being educated. They are attending school, dressing in modern ways, joining the church, being civilized. They are proving to the world that the 'dog of the Kalahari' can, if given the opportunity, take his place with the other peoples of the world and have a share in the future of the Republic of Botswana.

9

OLD DOCTORS OF THE DESERT

I was sitting by our camp-fire far from any village on one of our medical tours. It was late evening with darkness coming rapidly down, when presently, along the track over which we had travelled, came a small wiry old man with stick in hand and blanket thrown over his shoulder. He stopped and chatted with us for a while. We were in lion country and I asked him if he was not afraid to travel alone through such country. He said, 'No, indeed, I am not afraid. A lion can only attack me if it is sent by witchcraft by an enemy. I am a Tswana doctor and there is no other doctor around here who is more powerful than I, so no harm can come to me.'

This belief in witchcraft is very common among the Batswana, although, with the great drive for education and with the turning to Christianity of many people, its importance in the lives of people is less than in former days. I have often discussed this question of witchcraft with educated people such as ministers, teachers, and nurses, and I find that for most of them the spirit world is very real and that witchcraft is a power that still influences the lives of people.

Many happenings, such as accidents, illness, and sudden death, are accounted for by witchcraft. The Tswana doctors, of whom there are very many in every tribe in Botswana, are associated with evil spirits and evil powers. It is a widely held belief that certain people, especially some Tswana doctors, have the power after dark to turn themselves into witches, known as *baloi*. These *baloi* appear as ordinary people during the day, but at night, changing into evil spirits, can enter houses when people are asleep and inject poison into their bodies. They can put poison in food, and they can even put a person into a deep sleep and then travel long distances riding upon that person's back. That explains why sometimes a person wakes up in the morning stiff and sore. They have been taken for a ride by witches!

I have several friends and acquaintances among the witch-doctors, whom we prefer to call Tswana doctors. They seem to diagnose and heal in three different ways, and most of the doctors I know use two or more of these methods. One method is to throw the bones of divination; another is to suck out disease from the patient's body; the third is by the use of herbs. They are usually jolly fellows who love to boast about their powers to divine and to heal. They are expert psychologists and know just how their patients will react, and they know the exact word to say to each patient.

Certainly old Nkale is the most conceited I have yet met. He usually brings his three wives to me when they are ill, and several times I have visited his lands to help his daughters in labour. When I ask him for four shillings he loves to put his hand in his inside jacket pocket and bring out a wad of notes. He will choose one carefully and then, with a careless, 'Keep the change,' throw the note down on my desk. Then very deliberately he will wrap the wad of notes up again, returning it to his pocket with an expression which clearly says, 'You know, you really do not know how to make money!' One day I introduced him to some American visitors of mine who asked him about his occult powers. He really let himself go and I had never realized that he claimed such powers!

'If I wished, I could cause the doctor's truck to have an accident on the road. I can send lightning to strike an enemy. I can send sickness three hundred miles to an enemy in Johannesburg so that he will die there. I can cause a man's cattle to die, his crops to fail, and his wife to die in childbirth.'

We listened spellbound to his list of powers, and at the end we were relieved when he smiled kindly and said, 'Of course, being the good man I am, I would never dream of using my power in these ways; rather do I use it to cure diseases and to bless weddings and new houses.'

One day, I was walking through a small village with the local pastor and as we passed some huts I looked over the low wall of the courtyard. A group of people were sitting in a half circle and a Tswana doctor was throwing his divination bones. The pastor and I leaned over the low wall, listening. No one seemed to mind. All eyes were on the doctor.

'He is finding lost money,' explained the pastor to me.

It appeared that the old granny, whom I saw watching the doctor very carefully, had placed a purse containing a few shillings on the top of her hut wall, just beneath the thatch roof. The day before, when she went to take her purse she could not find it. Someone had removed it from its hiding-place. All who lived in the courtyard, her two sons and their wives and several children, denied all knowledge of the money and all expressed great regret that she had been robbed. The old lady, determined to find her money, had called the Tswana doctor to help her. He had just thrown his bones and was speaking to them at great speed as they lay in front of the silent people. He picked them up and threw them several times, touching them lightly and talking to them all the time. Suddenly he was silent. He turned to the old lady, conscious that all eyes were upon him and all ears open.

'The money is not far away, Granny. It has not left this courtyard. It has not yet been spent. But I am very sorry for the person who has hidden the money for it will bring him bad luck. Your money will be found; do not doubt, it will come back.'

The assembled people looked at each other and, mumbling softly, they gradually rose and left the courtyard.

The pastor chuckled. 'He is a clever old doctor, that! She'll have her money returned to her. He is pretty sure that the money is still around, hidden by one of the children. He has now scared the life out of the culprit, who, when night comes, will quietly return the purse to its place!'

I never heard if the money was returned or not, but I realized again that the Tswana doctor was a good psychologist who understood his own people!

Kelepang is a famous Tswana doctor, who still, I believe, practises his trade in a village just outside the Bakwena area. What a lovable old rascal he looked lying there in the hospital bed with his long white beard on top of the red blankets! He had been a pathetic figure a few days previously when the police had brought him to hospital after he had staggered into the village of Ga-Thamaga.

Kelepang was a good seventy years of age and his prostate gland was enlarging rapidly. The result was that one cold wet day he found that he was unable to pass his water. He struggled with this inconvenience for two days and nights, and then the agony of a hugely distended bladder drove him to seek help in his village. His wife saw the glazed look in his eye, the pinched mouth, the dirty tongue, and called the Headman who wisely informed the police. Within an hour of his admission to hospital, the dejected and ill doctor had a tube inserted in his bladder, which relieved his distress and made life bearable again. In a couple of days Kelepang was more like his old self again. His deep black eyes shone in his face like brightly burning coals and his white, pointed beard gave his face a mischievous and rather evil look. He was the life and soul of the ward and thrilled the patients with his stories and legends every evening.

I removed his prostate gland under spinal anaesthesia. I chatted to him as I poked my forefinger deep into his bladder and hooked out a prostate gland the size of a grape-fruit. Kelepang looked at it intently as I held it up for him to see. 'Ugh,' he said, 'some strong witch-doctor has bewitched me for that thing to grow. Still you white doctors are clever chaps. I'll soon recover now.' And he did. In a day or two he was walking about the ward and passing his water normally.

ALMOST PERSUADED

One morning on the ward round I found a boy of about fourteen years of age lying not far from the old man's bed. This child had a high fever and was unable, because of fever and weakness, to pass his urine. Sister said that for long she had been trying to help the boy, but it looked as if I would have to come and catheterize him.

Suddenly old Kelepang jumped out of bed. 'I'll help him,' he cried; and the light of battle was in his eye! He was eager to show his power. 'There is a plant I have seen growing just outside the ward. I'll make an infusion of the roots of it and I'll give some to the boy, and within half an hour he will pass his urine.'

The old man sounded so confident that I gave him permission to try. The old man was out of the ward in a flash and quickly dug up a little plant. He put the roots in a pot and boiled them on the kitchen stove. By the time I had finished the ward round, the brew was made and cool enough to drink.

'Come on, then,' I bantered, 'let us see what you can do!'

Kelepang stretched himself up to his full height. His gaunt figure, in the long hospital nightgown went tense, his left forefinger pointed up to the ceiling, his eyes were like piercing daggers, and in a loud voice he shouted: 'Now all you who watch, bear witness; if it is God Almighty's wish, when I have given this medicine to the boy, he will, after a short time pass his urine.'

There was a great hush in the ward. All eyes were on the witch-doctor. He handed the pot to the boy saying, 'Drink it all.' The boy gulped down the brownish fluid, while Kelepang went back to his bed where he sat watching the boy with eyes aflame and mouth firmly set. There was silence in the ward for a full five minutes, and then suddenly the patient yelled out, 'Nurse give me a urinal!' Never did a nurse move so quickly! Kelepang grinned his mischievous grin and turned over in his bed.

He was almost persuaded to become a Christian, but the hold of a lifetime of evil and witchcraft was too much for him. He found that the price he had to pay would be too great. He asked to speak privately to Rev. Andrew Kgasa and me one day. Those eyes of his pierced mine and that intent look came on his face again. 'God has spoken to me. You have been very good to me. I came here almost dead and now I am well again. God is calling me to become a Christian. I will follow Jesus Christ.'

We talked with him and we prayed with him and we could hardly believe our ears. The next day he produced some money to buy a Bible, and day by day when we did the ward round we found him sitting up in bed reading the Bible. But as his physical strength returned I had a feeling that his enthusiasm for the Christian way was becoming less ardent. I knew what the real test of his sincerity was and I waited for the day of his discharge before finally testing him. When he came into hospital I had taken from his locker his witch-doctor's bones, a dozen or so small bones, with a few marbles and some decorated pieces of plastic material, all in a small cotton bag. I held them up before him and said, 'Well, you will not be needing these bones of divination now, so I'll just keep them here.' His face contorted; his hand shot out. 'I need them, I need them,' he shouted. He saw the look of disappointment on my face and reluctantly he said, 'Oh, all right, keep them.' But I knew that, like the rich young ruler in the gospel, he had failed the test, the price was too great. I watched him walk proudly down the hospital road. At the gate he turned and waved once and then was gone and back to his witchcraft he went.

THE BLOOD SUCKER

Kgosiemang was a different kind of Tswana doctor who specialized in 'sucking out' diseases. The first time I saw him at work I was quite revolted, although fascinated, and I noted that the psychological effect on his patient was tremendous. Kgosiemang is a Mokgalagadi and they and the Masarwa have developed this type of treatment to a fine art.

I found him at work at the back of some huts when I was visiting some patients. His patient was a young married woman whom I suspected of having tuberculosis. She was sitting cross-legged, with blouse removed, on the floor, together with her husband and the doctor. The doctor was dressed in an old tattered shirt and a pair of buckskin trousers; his heavy face was deeply lined and his hands filthy with long nails full of dirt. His only instrument was a small knife, home-made out of a piece of tin, and sharp as a razor at its rounded end. He used the palm of his hand as a strop for the knife.

The woman showed him where she felt the pain, in front of her chest and between the shoulder blades. The doctor palpated the areas of pain with his rough, gnarled fingers, and then plucking the skin of the woman's chest up between finger and thumb, he made a small incision into the skin. This he repeated at four places. Each cut was just deep enough to draw blood and was about half an inch long. The doctor then put his mouth over the first cut and began to suck. As he sucked the woman's skin became elongated into his mouth. He pressed his lips hard on her chest to obtain a better grip. He sucked with all his strength, and began to breathe heavily, and the veins on his head and neck stood out like cords. He began to grunt and groan and eventually he must have exerted several pounds of pressure with his suction. The pain must have been quite severe but the woman sat impassive and motionless. After sucking for a good minute the doctor slowly let go and the skin came slowly out of his mouth. Then on to an old piece of tin which was lying nearby the doctor spat out the contents of his mouth, some saliva, a good deal of blood, and some little pieces of fleshy-looking material. He then repeated the sucking process over each of the cuts he had made.

He had certainly succeeded in performing a cupping which would have satisfied British physicians of an earlier generation! I noticed, however, that it was only at the first cupping that anything solid was sucked out. In the other places the doctor succeeded merely in producing blood and saliva. After completing his sucking the doctor produced a tin of black ointment, made I think from axle grease, and this he liberally applied to the cuts, after blowing away the numerous flies which had beaten him to the bleeding spots.

Kgosiemang now picked up a twig and called husband and wife to examine closely the results of his efforts. He probed with the twig in the now congealed mass of blood and saliva and fished out a small piece of bone and two small pieces of meat. Husband and wife gazed in horror at these pieces and asked what they could be.

Kgosiemang had his answer ready, 'The bone is part of a human bone and the two pieces of flesh are pieces of human placenta. You have been poisoned with these by an enemy. Still, now they are out, you will recover.'

The woman's face, which had been expressionless up till this point, now broke out into a broad smile and her husband, who had been morose and glum all through the treatment, also smiled and willingly paid the doctor a goat for his fee. I wanted to ask the doctor how it was that he only managed to suck the flesh out of the first cut, as I suspected that he had the pieces of flesh hidden in his mouth before he started; but I was anxious about the woman whose appearance I did not like. So I said to the husband, 'If she is still ill after a week, bring her to me for X-ray.' He brought her the next week and the X-ray showed extensive tuberculosis of both lungs.

Slowly but surely, the influence of the traditional doctor, with his priest-like influence over all aspects of life, is waning. More and more of the younger people are losing faith in him and his methods, and I think it is only a matter of time before the witch-doctor is a thing of the past. But it will take time. Every village today has its traditional doctors who are concerned, not only with healing, but with cleansing after childbirth and abortion, with blessing marriage ceremonies, blessing new houses and lands, treating cattle and small stock for infertility, and cleansing relatives after deaths.

The traditional doctor with his witchcraft provides a link for many people with the occult and with the great spirit world around. Occasionally such a traditional Tswana doctor will become a Christian, and when that happens I always notice how pleased the Christians are, a pleasure that is often tinged with a little doubt as they know how hard it is for such a man to give up a lucrative practice. Yet give it up he must if he is to follow Christ, for many of his practices are evil and full of superstition.

IO

FIRST SPEAKER OF BOTSWANA

In May 1960, while on leave in Scotland, I received a cable from the British Resident Commissioner Sir Peter Fawcus, asking if I would stand as a nominated member of the Legislative Council. I knew very little about politics; I was a missionary and a doctor, and I was a little afraid of dabbling in politics. I discussed the matter with my wife, and the mission authorities in Scotland, and then I cabled back that I would be willing to stand. I was into politics in a mild and gentle way. I missed the official opening of the Legislative Assembly on June 20, 1961, when Sir John Maud, as High Commissioner, launched the infant council on its voyage towards the ultimate goal of a fully representative independent National Assembly of Botswana. I took my seat in November 1961.

In 1962 Sir Peter asked me if I would accept the post of Speaker. I was staggered and I stalled, saying how little I knew of parliamentary procedure. Presently he said, 'You know, it was Seretse Khama who suggested you for the job.' That settled it and I said, 'I will give it a trial.' Next week Sir Peter came to Molepolole and we spent a day together going through 'standing orders' of the Legislative Council and discussing points of procedure. I felt like a student again, and I lay awake at night trying to understand and then memorize 'standing orders'. My favourite textbook had always been Price's *Textbook of Medicine*; now it became Erskine May's *Parliamentary Procedure*.

Then came 1963, the year of destiny for Bechuanaland; the year of the census of all the people; the year of great political activity; the second year of drought; the year of uncertainty and fear for the future. Above all it was the year of Sir Seretse Khama's gradual rise to national leadership. Child of Khama! What a heritage! Grandson of the great Chief Khama, one of the greatest, the kindest, the strongest, the most able, and the most devoutly Christian of all African Kings, Seretse had come back from exile in Britain with a vision of a united independent Botswana, and by his skilful leadership achieved his aim.

The British Government announced the date of the first General Election. It was to be March 1, 1965.

SERETSE TAKES OVER

The Democratic Party issued an election manifesto in which Seretse Khama's policy for the development of the country was set out. This was a far-sighted and impressive document, showing great powers of leadership. The Party promised to develop educational and medical services, and to encourage people of all races to work together for the good of the country. As election fever rose, it became obvious that the country as a whole, especially the more responsible people, were turning to the Democratic Party which won an over-whelming majority.

I wondered if I would still be required as Speaker of the National Assembly. A few days before the first Legislative Assembly, in March 1965, was due to meet in the High Court in Lobatsi, the Prime Minister let me know that he still wanted my services, and that he was intending to propose my name for election by members of the Assembly as Speaker. The Constitution allowed the Speaker to be elected from out-side the members of the National Assembly. I waited outside the Assembly, feeling excited, tense and somewhat nervous. The gallery of the High Court was packed with invited officials, chiefs, heads of departments, and notable residents of all races. The members of the first elected national assem-bly were sworn in by the clerk, and then suddenly the door opened and the clerk, Godfrey Matenge, came to tell me that I had been elected Speaker unanimously.

I was thrilled! The first Speaker of a newly elected Assem-bly which was to manage the affairs of the country during this year of internal self-government. I entered the Assembly and, before taking the chair, I spoke from the House. I thanked the Assembly for entrusting me with such an exalted

91

post and I promised that, with God's help, I would maintain the dignity of the House and be quite impartial in all my rulings. Knowing that the Opposition consisted of only three members, I promised to safeguard the rights of the minority.

A NEW CAPITAL RISES

During all these momentous days, a new capital town was rising out of the virgin bush at Gaberones. Britain financed the project and sent expert planners and architects to do the job well. An earth wall nearly a mile wide dammed up the Notwani river-bed and after a few heavy showers of rain a dam nearly seven miles long was created. Long before the new town was built its water supply was ensured. Mighty bulldozers came to clear the bush, and instructions were given, wisely, that any indigenous tree of any size should be saved if at all possible. Sites were booked on a huge plan of the new capital by religious denominations for their future churches, by a few firms for business premises, and by individuals for houses. The plan showed that the new town would spread out fan-shaped from an apex, where the National Assembly building would be erected.

By the end of 1965 the new town was taking shape. The National Assembly building stands aloof, dignified and quiet, except for the soft splash of its fountains in the garden, between the main Chamber and the members' rooms. In front, a covered way of concrete arches connects the main Chamber with the other rooms, and to reach the large, copper entrance doors, one crosses a small moat of clear water, which is in circuit with the water of the fountains. The interior of the Chamber is plain, simple, impressive. The ceiling is high, the walls panelled wood, the windows slant to let in subdued sunlight, the floor is of thick dark green linoleum, and the visitors' gallery stretches round the back and two sides of the chamber. The Speaker's Chair is on a raised dais with the clerks' table in front, on which are the two dispatch boxes presented to the old Legislative Council by the British government.

Trinity Church represents a bold attempt at a united Christian witness in Gaberones. We, who were involved in the spiritual needs of the new capital—and I was involved because for years I had conducted a monthly service in English for Gaberones' whites—were appalled at the idea of a row of tiny buildings all struggling to keep alive a Christian witness. In our mind's eye we saw little Congregational, Presbyterian, Baptist, Methodist churches all side by side, with an Anglican church not far away. After much prayer and discussion between the various church leaders, the idea evolved of a united church to serve the new town. At first this idea was confined to non-Anglicans, and then the Anglican church asked to join in the venture. Some of us had hoped that the Anglicans would have been able to go the whole way to form one united congregation with a united Communion service. That, however, was going too far; so now, two separate congregations worship in Trinity church, the Anglicans and the Union Church of non-Anglicans.

All the denominations represented in this venture gave towards the building of the church, and the World Council of Churches made a substantial grant towards the project. Two broad-minded young men work together as leaders of the Church. The Rev. Alan Butler is the Anglican priest, while the Rev. Derek Jones, Congregational, is the non-Anglican minister. The Rectory and the Manse stand side by side, identical houses, next to the church. The two leaders have as their motto, 'Let nothing be done separately that can be done together.' The result is that, apart from the Anglican Communion Service, the rest of the services are really ecumenical. This is indeed an interesting venture, worthy of a new capital city, but only time will tell whether Trinity church will be able to deal effectively with the spiritual needs of multiracial, multi-denominational Gaberones. Roman Catholics have their splendid Cathedral of Christ the King.

Schooling has always been a problem in Botswana. In the old days there were separate primary schools for whites and Africans. Such a state of affairs could not be in the new town, and so Thornhill School was built. The medium of teaching is the English language and the school is open to all children whose knowledge of English is good. The school has a great prestige value among the people of Gaberones and it seems that nowadays children are being admitted whose knowledge of English is very limited. Gaberones Secondary School is so far growing rapidly. Under the able Headmaster, Ian Russell, assisted by a good staff of African and British graduates and some British volunteers, the standard of education is as good as that given in the well-established Catholic School at Khale and the Congregational School at Moeding. In spite of the growth of these schools there are still hundreds of children who cannot find a place in secondary schools.

So, in the eventful years of 1965 and 1966, the town grew and began to have its own character. It stands there, a town of new buildings, of open spaces, of attractive houses. Its atmosphere is developing, as the wives of ex-patriates water their gardens of flowering shrubs and brilliant zinnias and enjoy their sundowner parties in the evenings; as the wives of African politicians and civil servants learn to cook on electric stoves and hang pictures on the walls of their houses; as Indian traders entice a people moving from a subsistence economy to a monetary one to spend their money on dresses, clothes and household utensils; as hard-headed British and South African businessmen develop new industries, garages, hotels, petrol depots, repair shops, electric shops, and a hundred other small developments. The sun-baked town has a lazy, happy atmosphere, as black and white wander through the shops together. But the ex-patriates sometimes grumble and say, 'They are putting us out too quickly,' and the crowds of half-educated youths who have drifted to Gaberones from all over the country loiter and drink and plan that one day they will have jobs. This is Seretse's Town, built by the British, built for people of all races.

THE COMING OF INDEPENDENCE

Friday, September 30, 1966, was Independence Day. The wind had dropped, but the sky was grey with low clouds. All along the Mall and from every building hung the new flag, and blue, black, and white bunting was draped from every building. From the scaffolding above the half-built Trinity church a flag was flying. By 8 a.m. I was at Parliament Building where I was delighted to find that the Speaker's gown had arrived from the makers in London. I had begun to despair of its arriving in time. I tried it on, proudly, carefully. It was impressive, black silk with borders of blue and white to match the flag. At half past eight I took the Chair, entering the House proudly in the new gown as the clerk led the procession in through the main door. Commencing with myself as Speaker, we all took the oath of allegiance to the President and the Republic. The three opposition members held the Bible as we all did, but muttered their allegiance in soft, inaudible voices. This, I was later told, was a way of expressing their disapproval of the new régime.

Botswana is growing—the circle of love, of understanding, of mutual trust, together with the circle of development and progress. Young volunteers have come from Britain, the Peace Corps from America, and with the enthusiasm of youth they are throwing themselves whole-heartedly into the service of Botswana; building schools and clinics, teaching mathematics and Shakespeare, and helping to organize co-operative movements. And the youth of Botswana respond to the challenge of youth; youth works with youth and the circle enlarges; trust, progress, and development are seen on every side.

The mighty mining magnates have also come, with all their wealth and skill. Up in the north at Orapa they have found diamonds, copper, and nickel, and their powerful drills are pounding away at treasure stores hidden for generations under the deep Kalahari sands. Soon a new town will spring up, different from quiet Gaberones, a town of mines and shops, of trade unions and politicians, of big businessmen, of squatters and labourers, of co-operative movements, of churches united and disunited. A busy, bustling town of many races. Then the circle will enlarge and this circle of co-operation and love and trust between the races will be stretched to its limit, but, if all the races try and all the people aim for racial peace, the circle will not break; it will only grow larger so that neighbouring countries will marvel and wonder.

TO RESPECT, TO UNDERSTAND, TO LIVE

President of the Republic of Botswana

The pen of Sir Seretse Khama moved slowly across his page. He was sitting at his beautiful wooden desk, the gift of the Republic of South Africa; his face was set and his thoughts were heavy as he sought to urge his people to enlarge the circle of progress and racial harmony.

'We must all strive to respect and understand each other, so that white Batswana and black Batswana may live together in peace and love. We must all strive to live together so that Botswana, poor though she may be, will be an example to the whole of Africa of racial peace and harmony.'

The President walked to the window and looked out. His job was hard. The white people are so impatient and often aggressive, and the black people are often so jealous, and the politicians speak words of discord. The task before him is great: to build up this aracial society where every man is respected and where every man respects his neighbour; but if this task can be accomplished anywhere in Africa it can be done in Botswana. So he faces the task, determined to succeed, and in his veins runs the blood of Khama the great, giving him strength, will-power, and the ears of a people who still, humbly, reverently, look to the Great Duiker, the Chief, the President of the Republic of Botswana, for help and leadership.